FOREWORD

Blind children need the best education we can provide to enable them to minimise the effect of their disability and to develop their powers.

Schools for the blind were among the earliest types of special school to be provided in this country, largely by voluntary bodies. For many years, however, the education of the partially sighted was restricted in the mistaken belief that sight would deteriorate through excessive use. Only in recent years have a more broadly-conceived pattern of education for these children and the necessary supporting services begun to emerge.

But there still remained many problems requiring attention when this Committee was appointed. It has investigated them concisely but thoroughly. Decisions have not yet been taken on any of the recommendations addressed to the Government; they will need to be discussed with a range of interested bodies. I do not think there could be a better stimulus to discussion than the ideas contained in the report, and I know that everyone concerned with education for the visually handicapped will be indebted to Professor Vernon and her colleagues.

Margaret Thatcher

THE RT HON MARGARET THATCHER MP

Dear Secretary of State

1 We were appointed in October 1968 by your predecessor with the following terms of reference:

"to consider the organisation of education services for the blind and the partially sighted and to make recommendations."

2 We have a variety of backgrounds. These include the education of blind, partially sighted and fully sighted children; psychology; medicine; the administration of local education and health services; and the training of teachers of handicapped children. None of us, as members of the Committee, represents any organisation; our views are our own. In addition, two members are parents of blind or otherwise handicapped children, and two (as well as one assessor) are themselves blind. Their presence has materially helped us to remember that in our deliberations we have been concerned not with abstractions but with the well-being of children and families.

3 At the start we invited interested organisations and individuals, including the head teachers of all special schools for the visually handicapped, to submit written evidence on the basis of a statement of the main issues that we thought needed to be considered. Members of the public who wished to submit evidence were invited to do so through press announcements. A list of witnesses who responded to our invitations will be found in Appendix A. We were glad that some visually handicapped people and some parents of visually handicapped children were among them. After considering the written evidence we asked selected individuals to meet us for discussion of certain points.

4 We set up two working parties on the curriculum and organisation of schools for the blind and the partially sighted, which sent questionnaires to the schools. Members, either individually or in groups, visited the schools indicated in Appendix B, which lists all special schools for the visually handicapped. Several of our members and Miss Eira Clarke, a former headteacher of a Sunshine Home School, carried out at our request surveys of different aspects of education for the visually handicapped. Finally, Miss M. Robertson and Mr. M. J. Tobin made surveys for us of recent literature.

5 We were extremely grateful for the assistance we received throughout, for the trouble taken to answer our enquiries and for the kindness that we met with on our travels.

6 We wish to record our warm thanks to our Secretaries, Mrs P. Masters until September 1969 and thereafter Mr G. J. Sheppard, for the many tasks that they have so ably carried out for us, including the summarising of evidence and replies to questionnaires, and also for their patience and helpfulness. We are indebted too to Mr R. W. Chattaway and Mr G. H. Spencer, who in turn acted as Assistant Secretary to the Committee. Finally, we should like to express our appreciation of the advice and assistance which we received from the assessors from Government departments.

7 We now submit our report. The different professional approaches represented among the members of the Committee and its assessors have made it easier for us to recognise that the diverse needs of visually handicapped children can be satisfied only on a multi-disciplinary basis, involving education, psychology, medicine and social work. Our main endeavour has been, on the one hand, to ensure that the special requirements of both the blind and the partially sighted are met; and, on the other hand, to break down outmoded barriers where they exist—for example, between the education of visually handicapped and of sighted children, between visually handicapped children and their homes, and between teachers in schools administered by voluntary bodies and the main-stream of their profession. Our recommendations are designed to extend the opportunities open to visually handicapped children and to enable them to lead richer and fuller lives.

M. D. Vernon (Chairman)

Mary H. Bonham
M. S. Colborne Brown
D. Cook
Geoffrey Exley
Richard C. Fletcher
Caroline J. Fryd
B. G. Gretton-Watson
R. Gulliford
C. R. Harris
D. A. Jarvis
J. Kell
G. H. Marshall
M. C. Murray
H. Pigott
Vernon Smith
D. A. Watson
M. Williams

G. J. Sheppard (Secretary)

MEMBERSHIP OF THE COMMITTEE

Professor M. D. Vernon (Chairman), Emeritus and formerly Professor of Psychology, University of Reading.

Miss M. H. Bonham, teacher at Condover Hall School, Shrewsbury.

Mr M. S. Colborne Brown, Education Officer, Royal National Institute for the Blind.

Dr D. Cook, Chief Education Officer, Devon County Council.

Mr G. Exley, Head Master, School for Visually Handicapped Children, Bridgend.

Mr R. C. Fletcher, Head Master, Worcester College for the Blind.

Mrs C. J. Fryd, MBE, parent of a handicapped child.

Dr B. G. Gretton-Watson, Principal School Medical Officer and County Medical Officer of Health, Cheshire County Council.

Mr R. Gulliford, Senior Lecturer, Birmingham University School of Education.

Mr C. R. Harris, parent of a visually handicapped child.

Mrs D. A. Jarvis, CBE, Head Mistress, Tower Hamlets Girls' Comprehensive School, London, E.1.

Mrs J. Kell, Head Mistress, John Aird School for Partially Sighted Children until December 1970 and from January 1971, Adviser in Special Education, Buckinghamshire County Council.

Mr G. H. Marshall, Head Master, Exhall Grange School, Coventry.

Mrs M. C. Murray, deputy Head Mistress, Redwell County Secondary School, South Shields.

Dr H. Pigott, Chairman, Henshaw's Society for the Blind.

Mr Vernon H. Smith, Consultant Ophthalmologist, Birmingham and Midland Eye Hospital.

Mr D. A. Watson, Solicitor, Vice-Chairman of the Royal National Institute for the Blind.

Miss M. Williams, formerly tutor to the Birmingham University Course for Teachers of the Blind.

ASSESSORS

Mr G. I. Crawford, CBE, Department of Education and Science (until October 1970).

Mr M. A. Walker, Department of Education and Science (from November 1970).

Mr W. H. Snowdon, HM Inspector.

Dr S. R. Fine, Medical Officer, Department of Education and Science

Mr V. J. Harley, Department of Health and Social Security.

Miss S. West, Department of Health and Social Security.

Mr A. E. Wilson, OBE, Department of Employment.

Mr A. W. M. Heggie, Scottish Education Department (until August 1969).

Mr G. G. McHaffie, Scottish Education Department (from September 1969)

Mr A. Milne, HM Inspector, Scotland (from February 1970).

SECRETARIAT

Mrs P. Masters, Secretary (until July 1969).

Mr G. J. Sheppard, Secretary (from November 1969).

Mr R. W. Chattaway, Assistant Secretary (until January 1970).

Mr G. H. Spencer, Assistant Secretary (from February 1970).

The estimated cost of the production of the report is £31,492, of which £1,548 represents the estimated cost of printing and publication, £24,049 the cost of administration and £5,895 the travelling, subsistence and other expenses of members.

CONTENTS

Appendices

CHAPTER 1 : INTRODUCTION

HISTORICAL REVIEW

1.01 The education of the blind has a long and honourable history in this country. It is however recorded elsewhere and we will mention only a few major landmarks. In 1791 a school was opened in Liverpool where the blind would be instructed in 'Music or the Mechanical Arts, and so be rendered comfortable in themselves, and useful to their country'. By the end of the 18th century it had been followed by three more institutions in Bristol, Edinburgh and London. At this period institutions for the blind tended to combine several of the functions of providing education for children, training them for industrial occupations, providing employment for some adults and giving shelter to the aged. In 1829 Louis Braille invented what is still the main medium of reading and writing for blind children, and its general adoption in the second half of the 19th century was a big educational advance. All the pioneer work for the blind was carried out by voluntary bodies, and an important development was the foundation in 1868 of the British and Foreign Blind Association, later to become the Royal National Institute for the Blind.

1.02 The early schools for the blind were residential. The first day special classes for the blind were opened in 1878 by the London School Board. In 1885 the State took a hand: a Royal Commission on the Blind, Deaf and Dumb was set up, which was the first and also—until we were appointed—the only Government enquiry which covered the whole field of the education of the blind[1]. The general approach of the Commission seems, to the modern mind, typically Victorian:

> " The blind, deaf and dumb, and the educable class of imbeciles form a distinct group, which, if left uneducated, become not only a burden to themselves, but a weighty burden to the State. It is in the interest of the State to educate them, so as to dry up as far as possible the minor streams which ultimately swell the great torrent of pauperism . . . It cannot be said that the group spoken of are as a rule impoverished by any fault of their own; to deal with them, therefore, liberally in such matters as education or out-door relief cannot be viewed as offering any reward to vice, folly or improvidence."

1.03 On the other hand, several of the Royal Commission's conclusions in its report in 1889 were very enlightened. For example, at a time when the minimum school leaving age was 10, it recommended compulsory education for blind children between the ages of 5 and 16; and, on the question whether blind children are better educated with the seeing, it remarked:

> " The free intercourse with the seeing gives courage and self-reliance to the blind, and a healthy stimulus which enables them to compete more success-

---

[1] The report of the Departmental Committee on the Welfare of the Blind, set up by the President of the Local Government Board in 1917, had 5 pages on the education of the blind, largely in the context of preparation for industrial or professional training.

1

fully with the seeing in after life than those who have been brought up al-together in blind institutions."

The report of the Royal Commission led to the Elementary Education (Blind and Deaf Children) Act 1893, which laid upon local school boards the duty of ensuring that blind and deaf children in their areas received a suitable elementary education; and for these children education was made compulsory from the age of 5 to 16. By the Education Act 1902 the functions of school boards were transferred to larger local education authorities. In the Education Act of 1921 the blind were one of the only 4 categories of handicapped pupils mentioned by name.

1.04 Special education for the partially sighted developed very much later. Until the end of the 19th century these children were educated either in ordinary schools on the same lines as fully sighted children, or in schools for the blind by methods similar to those used for blind children. A real differentiation in the methods of teaching the blind and the partially sighted was first made in 1907, when the London County Council provided instruction in reading and writing through large print to children in their schools for the blind who suffered from high myopia. Nottingham adopted a similar policy in the same year. In 1908 the LCC established at an elementary school the first special class for high myopes and children suffering from severe degrees of defective vision. This class was followed by others in London, but by 1930 nearly all the special provision made for the partially sighted was in day special schools (one notable exception was Liverpool). The education provided was very much restricted by the strong belief of many ophthalmic advisers that the reading of print had a damaging effect upon the myopic eye; and other partially sighted children, whose condition was stationary, were treated in the same way for fear of setting a dangerous example.

1.05 In 1931 the Board of Education appointed a Committee, with Dr R. H. Crowley, the Board's Senior Medical Officer, as Chairman, " to inquire into and report upon the medical, educational and social aspects of the problems affecting partially blind children." The following were among the main conclusions and recommendations in the Committe's report, which was published in 1934:

   (i) 'partially sighted' is a more appropriate term than 'partially blind';

  (ii) partially sighted children should not, as a general rule, be sent to schools for the blind;

 (iii) when possible, partially sighted children should be educated in classes forming an integral part of elementary schools;

 (iv) for the benefit of children in rural and small urban areas where day special classes would be impracticable, the Board of Education should consider a reorganisation of the residential blind schools so as to set some apart for partially sighted children only; and

  (v) the prevailing practice of prohibiting reading (except from very large hand-printed type) should be relaxed for myopes and abandoned for other partially sighted children. Restrictions on work under artificial light and on physical training could also be relaxed.

2

1.06 Little change took place in the arrangements for, and methods of education of, partially sighted children in the years immediately following the Crowley Report. Two reasons for this were suggested in the report of the Chief Medical Officer of the Ministry of Education (' The Health of the School Child ') for 1946 and 1947:

" The first was that, since the number of partially sighted children in the area of most urban Authorities was small—the proportion estimated by the Committee being 1 per 1,000—it seemed difficult for Authorities to make adequate arrangements for day schools, and combinations of Authorities to provide boarding schools were unusual. The second was that, despite the recommendations of the Committee regarding relaxation of some of the more severe restrictions imposed by ophthalmic advisers, the curriculum was so limited by prohibitions that some medical officers hesitated to condemn children to such a meagre intellectual diet, and preferred to leave them in ordinary schools, even though they were there making little progress. They certainly raised little agitation for an increased number of places."

1.07 Regulations[2] under the Education Act of 1944 made the partially sighted a separate category of handicapped pupils. The blind were defined as " pupils who have no sight or whose sight is or is likely to become so defective that they require education by methods not involving the use of sight;" and the partially sighted were defined as " pupils who by reason of defective vision cannot follow the ordinary curriculum without detriment to their sight or to their educational development, but can be educated by special methods involving the use of sight." The Act stimulated the review of old ideas and practices and encouraged developments in a number of directions. One or two examples will suffice. In 1945-47 four boarding special schools, previously used for both blind and partially sighted children, became the first boarding schools for the partially sighted only. All-age schools for the blind in the North of England were reorganised in the late 1940s, so that blind children there had to change school at the age of 11+. At this time too ophthalmologists in general changed their attitude to myopia.

CURRENT TRENDS AND PROBLEMS

1.08 At the time when we were appointed the world of education for the visually handicapped was beset by problems, causing some uncertainty of aim and anxiety about the future. In the special schools for the blind, there had been striking changes in the numbers and disabilities of their pupils. As a result of improved peri-natal care, numbers of children blind from birth have fallen considerably during this century. There was in the late 1940s and early 1950s a sudden increase due to the appearance of retrolental fibroplasia, a condition associated with excessive oxygen pressure given to premature babies; but the prevalence of this condition has now been greatly reduced and most of the children suffering from it have passed out of the schools. In the past a substantial proportion of blind children in schools were otherwise normal. Now

---

[2] The Handicapped Pupils and Special Schools Regulations 1945. The definition of partially sighted pupils has been slightly changed in the current version of the regulations, operative from 1959, by the substitution of " normal regime of ordinary schools " for " ordinary curriculum."

an increasing proportion are blind as a result of conditions producing other handicaps (from some of which children used to die); and in these cases blindness may be allied to physical defects and/or mental handicap.

1.09 The fall in the prevalence of blindness had led to numbers in certain schools becoming so small that they had ceased to be viable, and to uncertainty about the continuing viability of other schools, including the selective ones. This had naturally caused uncertainty among the staff and the bodies responsible for the schools. Small-scale experiments in ' integrated education ' for some of the most gifted blind children of secondary age, ie sending them by day to a local grammar or comprehensive school, had been viewed with apprehension. At the same time, across the whole range of special education increasing concern was being expressed about avoiding the segregation of handicapped children in a world apart and about keeping them in the closest possible touch with ordinary children.

1.10 Parents of blind children in the North of England were well aware that children in the South did not have to change schools at 11+ and go to one which might be some distance from their primary school; this had caused much dissatisfaction. At the same time, questions were being asked about the extent to which special schools ought to fall in line with trends in ordinary primary and secondary schools over issues such as all-age schools and selective education. For all children, whether handicapped or not, there was a growing belief in the importance for a child's development of preserving the bonds between him and his family, particularly in his earlier years. Parents of blind children often felt anxiety at the separation from home at a tender age and the distress it might cause. They deplored the scarcity of facilities for securing educational help and counselling if they kept their child at home until he was at least 5 years old. Indeed, parents even disliked having to send older children to boarding schools outside the region (as happened, for instance, in the South West of England, which by 1968 had no schools for the blind).

1.11 Because of the totality of their handicap blind children have always attracted much more sympathy, and their needs more attention, than the partially sighted. A wider range of special facilities is naturally needed for the more severe handicap, but there was a number of services and other kinds of provision for the blind the absence of which for the partially sighted was regarded by many people as a serious disadvantage. For instance, there were no social workers specially trained for work with the partially sighted; there was nobody like the RNIB to assist in providing suitable books and other services; teachers of the partially sighted were not required to hold an additional teaching qualification and there was no part-time course available for them; and there was no special centre to which school leavers could go for further education.

1.12 There was general dissatisfaction with the arrangements for the assessment and registration of visually handicapped children. There was uncertainty about the right point of division between schools for the blind and for the partially sighted, and about the desirability of transferring children between schools as their eye condition changed. At times schools for the blind and the partially sighted had been criticised by each other for retaining pupils who were better suited to the educational methods of the other type of school.

4

1.13 Some doubt was felt about whether schools both for the blind and for the partially sighted always employed the methods best suited to overcome the children's disabilities and to develop their skills. There was a serious shortage of books and of other equipment such as audio-visual aids and scientific apparatus. Finally, the vocational guidance of visually handicapped school leavers gave rise to certain difficulties.

1.14 This is not intended to be an exhaustive list; other problems which have not yet been solved will be mentioned in the course of our report. The chief development during the years when we have been at work has been the assumption in April 1971 by the Department of Education and Science and local education authorities of responsibility for the education of the severely mentally handicapped, some of whom may also have a visual handicap.

CHAPTER 2 : STATISTICS

2.01 Appendix C to this report contains the main statistical information which we have collected during our work. These statistics indicate the framework within which future educational provision for the visually handicapped must be made. We therefore begin by considering how much these statistics can tell us and—certainly no less important—how much they leave unsaid.

THE PRESENT POSITION

2.02 In January 1971 there were according to returns from local education authorities and schools 1,207 blind children and 2,338 partially sighted children either receiving education at special schools, independent schools, special classes and units or at home or awaiting admission to special schools. These 2 figures correspond to prevalence rates respectively of 1·37 and 2·66 per 10,000 school population. 97% of the blind and 42% of the partially sighted were boarding pupils. The totals include 50 blind and 33 partially sighted children aged under 5 awaiting admission to special schools.

2.03 To provide education for these pupils there are in England and Wales 18 special schools for the blind, 19 for the partially sighted and 2 for the blind and partially sighted together. The ages of the children in the schools are shown in Figures 1 and 2 of Appendix C. The following table gives the number of schools catering for different age-ranges:

Maintained By	Nursery & Infants			Primary			All-Age			Secondary			Totals			
	B	PS	B/PS	B	PS	B/PS	B	PS	B/PS	B	PS	B/PS	B	PS	B/PS	
LEAs	–	–	–	1	1	–	1	15*	1	–	–	–	2	16	1	19
Voluntary † organisations	6‡	–	–	3	–	–	2	3	1	5**	–	–	16	3	1	20
Totals	6	–	–	4	1	–	3	18	2	5	–	–	18	19	2	39
	6			5			23			5			39			

* One of these schools has a partially selective intake at the secondary stage.

† To distinguish them from schools maintained by local education authorities, special schools managed by voluntary organisations are known as non-maintained schools.

‡ These Sunshine Home schools normally take children up to 7 years old.

** Three of these schools are selective.

2.04 All the schools for the blind and 5 schools for the partially sighted are boarding schools (though in a few cases children who live nearby may attend as day pupils). All schools except 2 of the selective schools for the blind provide for both boys and girls. The 39 schools between them provide accommodation for up to 1,315 blind and 1,926 partially sighted pupils. There are also 3 establish-

6

ments for the further education and training of blind adolescents, also run by voluntary bodies, with 256 on roll in January, 1971; there are no such establishments for the partially sighted. In addition to the special schools for the visually handicapped, there are 9 schools for delicate or physically handicapped children which also have a partially sighted unit and 9 special classes for partially sighted children in 8 ordinary schools. There is also an unknown number of visually handicapped children in hospitals for the mentally handicapped and in the new special schools (previously junior training centres); as well as a further unknown number of children suffering from visual defects not all of which are so severe as to merit placement in a special school or class who are being educated in ordinary schools.

2.05 It will be seen from Figure 3 of Appendix C that the number of special school places available in each region does not always match the number of visually handicapped children living in that region. There are no places for blind children in the East Midlands, East Anglia and South West regions, but more places than children in the North West, West Midlands and other South East regions. (The move of Henshaws School from the North West to the Yorkshire and Humberside region in late 1971 distributes the places more evenly). For the partially sighted the imbalance is slightly less marked.

TRENDS

2.06 There are 2 basic sources of statistical information about recent trends which are relevant to future educational provision for the visually handicapped: educational statistics maintained by the Department of Education and Science and registers of handicap maintained by the Department of Health and Social Security. Each of these has disadvantages as a predictive source. The educational statistics relate to the numbers of blind and partially sighted children receiving and/or requiring special educational treatment at annual intervals, but do not supply any medical details of the precise nature of the handicaps concerned. They do not therefore allow full account to be taken of medical trends, such as fluctuations among particular causes of visual handicap, which may materially affect future special educational needs. The registers maintained by the DHSS are also unsatisfactory because registration is by no means universal and is often not effected until well beyond the actual date of onset of the handicap, even in the case of congenital defects. This makes correlation with educational statistics especially difficult. Registration is not a pre-requisite for special educational treatment (although in practice all children in schools for the blind would be registered), and thus the registers are an inadequate guide to future numbers in need of special schooling. Predictions based on either educational statistics or the registers of handicap suffer from the further disadvantage that no account can be taken of possible medical advances in the treatment or cure of particular types of visual handicap, nor of new causes of visual handicap which may unhappily arise at any time: an example was retrolental fibroplasia, which caused a sudden increase in visual defects among children born in the early 1950s.

2.07 Despite these limitations in our sources of information, we have spent some time considering statistical evidence of trends in visual handicaps. In particular, we asked the DES to project for us the numbers of children needing special educational treatment as a result of visual handicap. This they did on the basis of the actual numbers of visually handicapped children from 1961 to 1971 receiving and said to be requiring special education (see Figure 4 of Appendix C). These numbers revealed for blind children a downward trend over the whole decade due to the decline in retrolental fibroplasia. The figures for partially sighted children showed an unexplained drop from 1966-1967 and a slight increase over the decade as a whole. The projections for blind children suggested a continuing decrease in numbers to just under 1,000 children receiving and requiring special education in 1980, compared with 1,207 in 1971 and 1,448 in 1961. It would not be reasonable to continue such downward acceleration indefinitely, since there is inevitably a " floor " below which the figures are most unlikely to fall because of the continuing numbers of congenital defects. A curvilinear trend has therefore been fitted to the data and extrapolated towards an assumed floor or asymptote, which suggests a continuing total of about 1,000 children each year—or an incidence rate of 0·9 per 10,000. The 1966-1967 drop made projection of partially sighted numbers more tentative, but it was suggested that there might be an increase to about 2,630 partially sighted children receiving and/or requiring special education in 1980, compared with 2,338 in 1971 and 2,082 in 1961. These projections are, of course, subject to the considerations stated in paragraph 2.06.

2.08 Another difficulty is that the educational statistics of children receiving and/or said to be requiring special education do not derive from absolute unchanging standards of identification and assessment. The trends suggested by educational statistics from 1961 to 1971 may thus not necessarily reflect an actual decrease in numbers of blind children coupled with an increase in the numbers of partially sighted children. Since the partially sighted/blind borderline is not fixed rigidly, there may be a tendency to assess as partially sighted for educational purposes increasing numbers of children who might in the past have been assessed as blind. So far as the partially sighted are concerned, the educational figures may conceal improvements in the identification of partially sighted children and/or fluctuations in the extent to which partially sighted children are assessed as suitable for education in ordinary schools.

2.09 Although, as indicated, the figures for registration of visual handicap among young children are not reliable indications of the exact numbers of visually handicapped children likely to be in special schools in the future, they might be expected to indicate at least the direction of overall future trends. The figures for registration of young partially sighted children are particularly unreliable, because only about 30% of children aged 0-15 are registered before they are 5 years old. Nevertheless, the statistics for registration of 0 to 4 year olds do show an increase from 1963 compatible with the increase in the numbers of partially sighted children receiving and/or requiring special education projected from educational statistics (see Figure 5). The statistics for registration of young blind children occasion more difficulty. Over the whole period 1955 to 1970 there has been a reduction from 173 to 127 in registrations of children children aged 0 to 4, but a drop from 1957 to 1962 has been followed by a new peak from 1963 to 1968 (see Figure 6). This might be thought merely to reflect an increasing awareness of the importance of registering children at an early age;

but this cannot be the explanation because, among children aged 0 to 15 registered each year from 1955, the proportion aged 0 to 4 has—except in one or two years—remained fairly constant at between 56% and 60%. If the 1963-68 peak does correspond to an increase in the actual numbers of blind children, there could be a slight " bulge " in the numbers of children in special schools for the blind over the next 5 to 10 years, contrary to the trends suggested by extrapolating educational statistics alone. On the other hand, it is possible that much of any increase in the number of blind children may reflect an increase in the number with additional handicaps (see paragraph 2.10): most of these children would not go to schools principally for the visually handicapped.

2.10 The registers of the blind give a strong indication of a rising prevalence of dual or multiple handicap among children of school age. The Education (Handicapped Children) Act 1970 brought all children within the educational system, but figures for earlier years divided children aged 5 to 15 into those regarded as suitable for education at school and those not suitable. If the latter are taken to be children suffering from a severe mental handicap, the proportion of blind children with severe mental handicap rose from 25·2% in 1959 to 35·2% in 1970 (line B of Figure 7); and the proportion of those with additional defects other than severe mental handicap rose from 16·8% in 1959 to 23·8% in 1970 (line A). The total proportion of blind children with any additional handicap rose from 39·0% in 1959 to 50·6% in 1970 (line C). The registers of the partially sighted did not give this kind of information, but in 1969 one of our members carried out for us a survey of all partially sighted children in special schools for the visually handicapped and in classes or units attached to other schools (see Figure 8). This survey suggested that over 23% of partially sighted children then suffered from additional handicaps which were in themselves sufficient to warrant special educational treatment. Although we have no firm statistical data relating to a number of years, we believe that among the partially sighted as well as among the blind the prevalence of additional handicaps is an increasing problem.

CONCLUSIONS

2.11 Available statistics on visually handicapped children have proved difficult both to interpret and to extrapolate, and there have been instances where statistics for partially sighted children are less full than those for blind children. However, even given the inadequacy for our purposes of many of the available statistics, we think it fair to assume that special school places will need to be provided over the next decade for numbers of visually handicapped children as a whole which are most unlikely to fall below present levels unless there is some major advance in the prevention or cure of congenital visual defects. It also seems certain than an increasing proportion of these children will suffer from other defects in addition to their visual handicap.

RECOMMENDATION

2.12 We recommend that, for purposes of planning special school provision for the visually handicapped over the next decade, the total number of places required should be assumed to be approximately the same as at present.

9

CHAPTER 3 : MEDICAL SERVICES

3.01 In this Chapter we consider all aspects of medical services for visually handicapped children, both before they go to school and while they are at school. We have thus included the procedures of indentification, assessment and certification as well as the actual services, ophthalmic, other medical, psychiatric and psychological, provided in and for the school.

IDENTIFICATION, ASSESSMENT AND CERTIFICATION

The present position

3.02 Identification of a young child as possibly suffering from a visual handicap of some kind may be made at the hospital in which a child is born, by the general practitioner, at a child health clinic or by a health visitor. It is the responsibility in most cases of the general practitioner to arrange for the child to be examined by an ophthalmologist, unless special arrangements are made with general practitioners for referral direct from the child health clinic. There are very few places where whole population screening of very young children has been attempted. In Birmingham, however, an orthoptic screening service has been provided since 1967 by 4 sessions per week at child health clinics and, in particular, immunisation clinics. The numbers attending over the past 3 years were comparatively small: in 1970 only about 7% of the population aged 0 to 5 attended.

3.03 A visually handicapped child is usually referred to the local authority social services department by the health visitor or the hospital. Certification and registration of the handicap are voluntary, but are usually preliminaries to securing services and benefits. The condition is certified by a consultant ophthalmologist on the Department of Health and Social Security's Form BD8, obtained from the social services department which arranges and pays for the examination of the child. In the event of the child being certified as blind or partially sighted the social services department registers him as such. Although the Form includes assessment of the child's need for special educational treatment, the criteria to be applied in making the assessment are purely ophthalmological and the ophthalmologist is thus not required to consult other specialists, such as a paediatrician, psychiatrist or educationalist. Form BD8 is not completed until the age of 5 or over for about 42% of the children under 15 registered as blind each year. The corresponding figure for partially sighted children is 72%.

Evidence received

3.04 The Committe's letter inviting evidence asked specifically for views and comments on " the adequacy of the existing arrangements for the assessment and registration of visually handicapped children." Very few replies expressed any satisfaction with these arrangements. Frequently occurring criticisms were that many visually handicapped children slip through the net of existing identi-

10

fication arrangements; that the initial assessment of a child with a visual handicap should be made by a team of specialists rather than by an ophthalmologist alone; and that children should undergo regular re-assessment. It was also considered that, in both identification and assessment, consultation and co-operation are often poor between the various educational, health and social services agencies and, within the medical field, between the hospital eye service and the public health service.

3.05 Most of the evidence regarded Form BD8 as totally unsuitable for children. One trenchant comment was that Form BD8 " pays lip service only to assessment of a child's needs." Other criticisms made were that:

(i) Form BD8 is of little use for educational assessment;

(ii) it is often completed too late to enable parents to benefit from welfare services such as help in the home and advice on child management during their child's first few years;

(iii) it lays too much emphasis on visual acuity, which is not the sole determinant of a visually handicapped child's need for special education;

(iv) given the difficulties of assessment and frequent changes in many visual conditions, it draws too rigid a distinction between blind, partially sighted and normally sighted children and seeks to make too precise a prognosis; and

(v) it is of little or no value for assessing multiply handicapped children.

Consideration of the issues

3.06 We have been much impressed by the weight of the evidence that was strongly critical of the existing arrangements and we have carried out a radical re-appraisal of what is required. We attach the highest importance to the early detection of visual defects, since the earlier that treatment, training and parent counselling are started, the better is the ultimate prognosis for the child and his family. The early detection of handicapping conditions is therefore a major function of the modern child health service. The Department of Health and Social Security is encouraging the setting up of comprehensive assessment services for handicapped children. The object is to facilitate the assessment, by a multi-disciplinary team with members from the hospital and community services, of children with one or more handicaps, and their regular re-assessment in the light of their growth and development and of the effects of treatment, training, education and environment. A two-tier system is envisaged. Most of these children can be fully assessed in a centre at district level but a substantial minority are considered to require expertise and technical facilities available only at specialist regional centres. These will usually be associated with departments of child health, children's hospitals or departments which are part of a teaching hospital group. As the regional centre will provide a district service it will call upon the usual team for that purpose but a number of other specialists will be available. Although progress in establishing a comprehensive assessment service is expected to be slow, it is likely to be the pattern for the future and services on these lines are already being developed within the hospital provision in some areas. Elsewhere assessment services are being developed in centres outside the hospital where hospital and local authority staff and general practitioners can co-operate in the work of assessment.

11

3.07 It is obviously desirable that visually handicapped children in the same way as other handicapped children should participate in the general developmental assessment which will, it is hoped, eventually cover all children. Particularly as a considerable and increasing proportion of blind and partially sighted children suffer from other handicaps, it is also highly desirable that the visually handicapped should remain in contact with a comprehensive assessment team. The point however has been forcibly made to us that children with eye defects that are at all complicated require to be seen by an ophthalmologist with particular skill with, and interest in, children; and there is at present only a small number of these in the whole country. Furthermore, when a decision is needed on the special educational treatment required for a child, it seems more appropriate for the assessment for this purpose to take place in an educational than in a hospital setting.

3.08 We therefore envisage the process of identifying and assessing children with visual handicap operating on the following lines. If such a handicap was not suspected at birth, the first step would be the preliminary screening of all children for visual handicap at a child health clinic as part of the general development assessment.[1] Various attempts have been made to screen the whole of the pre-school child population specifically for visual handicaps, but results have not been encouraging. The numbers attending Birmingham's orthoptists' screening service, for example, were only a small proportion (about 7%) of those living within the catchment area. All parents should be expressly invited to submit their young children for general developmental assessment at child health clinics, and they should be encouraged to do so by health visitors and by suitable local publicity campaigns for the service. An appointments system should also help to increase attendance. Children picked out in the preliminary screening as possibly having a visual abnormality, or found at birth or by the family doctor or by the child health services to have an eye defect, would be referred for examination and any treatment required to the ophthalmologist who would be a member of a comprehensive assessment team based on a district general hospital. From this team the children would receive a general paediatric examination, including an assessment of developmental progress. The key members of the team would be a paediatrician, an ophthalmologist, a local authority medical officer with experience of handicapped children and, when he could participate, the child's general practitioner, together with an otologist, a health visitor and a social worker, and a psychiatrist or other experts as required. Wherever possible, a waiting room should be set apart at the district general hospital for children and their parents. The ophthalmologist of the comprehensive assessment team would notify a visual handicap to the local authority.

3.09 The ophthalmologist, after identifying the handicap and arranging treatment where appropriate, would refer any child with a significant visual handicap

---

[1] An estimate of the distance visual acuity can be achieved at any age, with varying degrees of accuracy. From infancy the Stycar tests (Sheridan 1968) are applicable and from an average of 2½ to 3 years the Sheridan Gardiner test, the E test of Albini, the Landolt ring test, and the Sjogren hand test are examples of tests available for the pre-school child. In cases where the existence of vision is in question the integrity and function of the visual pathway from globe to cerebral cortex can be established by electrodiagnostic means such as the electroretinogram and the electroencephalographic visual evoked response (VER).

for specialised ophthalmological/educational assessment to the special regional assessment centre. This would include as members of its team for this purpose an ophthalmologist with particular skill with, and interest in, children, an educational psychologist and a teacher of the visually handicapped. The educational psychologist would assess a child's psychological abilities at as early an age as was appropriate; he could appropriately be in the employment of a local education authority or voluntary body which maintained one of the principal schools for the visually handicapped in the region, and the teacher might be on the staff of the same school. A very few children will need to be given special tests (perhaps under an anaesthetic) the equipment for which will only be available in a hospital, but the members of the regional assessment team should ideally examine children in a school setting. Despite the shortage of paediatric ophthalmologists, the number of visually handicapped children requiring assessment in any year should not be so large as to require the ophthalmologists to spend an unacceptably large proportion of their time in the schools and thus away from their work in the hospitals. Moreover, the different members of an assessment team concerned with the child would not necessarily examine him at the same time, so long as they met for a case conference. After the regional assessment team had completed its work the members would then send a joint report back to the district assessment team. (Where a fully developed comprehensive assessment service did not yet exist, the ophthalmologist to whom a child was first referred and the paediatrician attached to the district general hospital would, between them, have to call in other specialists and arrange a case conference when the examination of a child had been completed).

3.10 In addition to this initial assessment by district and regional teams, all visually handicapped children should be re-assessed by the regional team at regular intervals of not more than a year. This is particularly important where there is any doubt about the initial assessment or where there is any likelihood that a child's visual acuity may change with time.

3.11 Parents should immediately be informed of their child's initial assessment, and of the services available to them for counselling (see Chapter 4) and child welfare. They should be advised as to the nature and consequences of the visual handicap, and as to the best means of assisting the child's development and his integration within the family group. They should be consulted about the child's educational placement, and should be continuously informed throughout his school life as to his condition and needs. Medical information should be presented to parents, in a form they can comprehend, by the specialist in conjuction with a trained social worker. The family doctor should be given an opportunity to be present at the assessment; in any event he should be fully informed of the results of the assessment and of the advice offered to the parents.

3.12 We agree with the evidence we received that Form BD8 is unsuitable for children. In many cases it cannot be filled in accurately until a child has reached his teens. It is a matter of urgency that a new form of notification should be introduced for use when a child is first identified as having a visual handicap (see Appendix D). We understand that the DHSS is consulting interested bodies, including the DES, about possible new arrangements for certification and registration. When boys and girls leave school at the age of 16, we consider that a form of certification will be necessary in relation to their capacity for employment, and this form might require alteration after vocational assessment and training have taken place.

OPHTHALMIC SERVICES IN ORDINARY SCHOOLS AND IN SPECIAL SCHOOLS FOR OTHER HANDICAPS

The present position

3.13 Screening of visual acuity for distance is carried out by nearly all local education authorities during the first year a child is at school. Returns made to the DES showed that in 1969 21 out of 164 local authorities in England and Wales made an annual review and many others carried out tests in alternate years, but in some areas re-testing is still infrequent. Children in whom abnormalities are suspected are referred for treatment either to school eye clinics or to hospital eye clinics, but ophthalmologists do not usually visit ordinary schools. Only in a few special schools for children with other handicaps (usually physical) are regular arrangements made for a consultant ophthalmologist to supervise the ophthalmic care of the children on the premises.

Evidence received

3.14 Our letter seeking evidence did not specifically ask about the adequacy of existing ophthalmic arrangements in ordinary schools. However, in commenting upon identification and assessment procedures, a number of those giving evidence mentioned the problem of identifying children placed in ordinary schools who had visual handicaps which had not previously been discovered. It was not generally thought that many blind children escaped the existing identification net, but many people considered that ordinary schools at present contained significant numbers of partially sighted children who would benefit either from special arrangements made for them in ordinary schools or from education in a special school for the visually handicapped. It was stated to us that of the 10 handicaps defined in regulations partial sight was one of the least understood by teachers.

Consideration of the issues

3.15 The arrangements for vision screening in schools are far from satisfactory. We consider it essential that vision screening of a high standard, including annual tests of visual acuity, should form part of the school health service, both in primary and secondary schools and in special schools for other handicaps (which may well include some children with partial sight), and it should be under the clinical guidance of an ophthalmologist. Where visually handicapped pupils are attending these schools the ophthalmic services for them must be of the standard provided in special schools for the visually handicapped. The importance of screening on entry to schools is emphasised by the poor response to the Birmingham Orthoptic Screening Service for children aged under 5, to which we referred earlier. As part of their training, all teachers (see Chapter 9), as well as all doctors, should be made aware of the problems of the visually handicapped and of the signs that a child may have a visual defect. In addition, all head teachers should be sent information and simple instructions

14

for their staff on the recognition of visual handicap, and all children suspected of this should be referred for medical examination. It would be most valuable if arrangements could be made for ophthalmologists to visit all special schools to carry out supervision of the children's eyesight.

OPHTHALMIC SERVICES IN SPECIAL SCHOOLS FOR THE VISUALLY HANDICAPPED

The present position

3.16 Most special schools for the visually handicapped have arrangements for their pupils to be seen regularly by an ophthalmologist. These arrangements are made privately in the majority of schools. A continuing watch, in most cases, is thus maintained on changes in the children's visual competence.

Evidence received

3.17 The Committee established 2 working parties to consider curriculum matters for blind and partially sighted children. In their questionnaires sent out to schools, both working parties asked how often the school ophthalmologist visited the school and whether he conferred with the head teacher, teachers and other specialists. Among schools for the blind the frequency of visits by the ophthalmologist varied from once a week to once a year, but most schools had a visit once a term and could arrange more frequent visits when they appeared to be needed. Among special schools for partially sighted children the evidence revealed a slightly different picture. The replies to the question about visits from the school ophthalmologist varied from weekly visits at 2 schools to "never" at one school. However, most of the schools have no difficulty in arranging visits when they appeared necessary.

Consideration of the issues

3.18 It is important that in all schools for the visually handicapped there must be regular and frequent visits from a consultant ophthalmologist who should be working for the National Health Service on a sessional basis. Good communication also is essential between him and the teaching staff, who should have access to relevant information from the medical records of the pupils. The facilities usually available to ophthalmologists at schools need improving. A suitable examination room could be equipped at the present time for approximately £2,000; the cost of this should be borne by the National Health Service. It is highly desirable that the ophthalmologist should, as part of his visual assessment, observe children at work and discuss them with the staff. We hope that the ophthalmologist in the special regional assessment team (see paragraph 3.09) will be able to act as the visiting consultant to special schools in the region.

3.19 Every school for the visually handicapped should be visited at least once weekly by an optician employed by the National Health Service on a sessional basis. He should work in close collaboration with the ophthalmologist in the supply and maintenance of spectacles and low visual aids. The prescription of all visual aids should be made through the Hospital Eye Service, and all pupils who need spectacles should have a spare pair.

3.20 We consider that many ophthalmologists are insufficiently informed about the identification and care of the visually handicapped child. It would be helpful if the Faculty of Ophthalmologists could consider ways of improving the position, e.g. by arranging visits to schools for the visually handicapped—which would be particularly useful for ophthalmologists during their training.

GENETIC COUNSELLING

The present position

3.21 Existing arrangements for genetic counselling of both the visually handicapped and parents with visually handicapped children are scanty. Apart from the Godfrey Robinson Memorial Unit for Ophthalmic Genetics, brought into being in 1963 by the RNIB at the Royal College of Surgeons, and the genetic clinic at Moorfields Eye Hospital, there are very few sources of professional advice, though some help is available to the visually handicapped from the 25 Genetic Advisory Centres organised by the hospital services in the various regions of England. It appears that relatively few ophthalmologists provide a widespread counselling service in ophthalmic genetics.

Evidence received

3.22 The studies have indicated that there is an extremely high prevalence of visual handicaps the aetiology of which suggests genetic origins. Of 776 visually handicapped children, most of whom were blind, included in a study[2] by the Godfrey Robinson Memorial Unit, over 40% had defects of genetic origin. This figure is supported by a survey made by Dr Fine,[3] one of the DES assessors, of children in special schools and classes for the visually handicapped. She found that in the 817 blind children studied, 22% of the defects excluding retrolental fibroplasia were identified as familial in origin and the aetiology of some others specified as unknown may have been hereditary. Of 1,374 partially sighted children, 34% were identified as having defects of familial basis, and this too can be considered an underestimate of those with abnormalities of genetic origin.

3.23 Since this statistical evidence had already been published when the Committee began to receive evidence, it was perhaps surprising that very little of the evidence received touched upon genetic counselling. The National Federation of the Blind in the UK expressed concern that visually handicapped children should at as early a stage as possible be warned of any foreseeable genetic consequences of their having children. Mr Alan Friedmann, who with Dr George Fraser was jointly responsible for the Godfrey Robinson Memorial Unit study, recommended to us the establishment of a central ophthalmic genetic unit which would examine all blind and partially sighted children in schools and would maintain a central register of as many people as possible of all ages in England and Wales who have a genetic visual handicap. An ophthalmologist with a special interest in genetic conditions was required to lead the central unit. On the other hand, Dr R. M. Forrester, Consultant Paediatrician to the RNIB, considered that genetic counselling was a matter of basic paediatrics.

---

[2] The Causes of Blindness in Childhood, 1969—Friedmann and Fraser.

[3] Education Survey No. 4—Blind and Partially Sighted Children, 1968 (HMSO).

16

Consideration of the issues

3.24 We consider that it is incumbent upon the ophthalmologist to see that genetic counselling is offered to parents and to older children. His aim should be to give a statement of the facts and of the risks involved in addition to advice. While at school children should also be informed where they will be able to obtain further genetic counselling once they have left school. In view of the clear evidence that the incidence of visual handicap could be reduced by the elimination of cases of genetic origin, we cannot overestimate the importance of making genetic counselling services available to all visually handicapped children and their parents.

3.25 We doubt whether a central ophthalmic genetic unit would meet the needs of the country as a whole and whether a central register is necessary. We think the right approach is, first, to arrange counselling in every region either through the ophthalmologist in the special regional assessment team or through the ophthalmologist in each comprehensive assessment team based in a district general hospital; and then in the light of experience to decide whether any centralised service is required.

PSYCHIATRIC & PSYCHOLOGICAL SERVICES

The present position

3.26 At present facilities are generally inadequate for psychiatric and psychological advice to parents and teachers of visually handicapped children and for psychiatric and psychological treatment where necessary for the children themselves. There are indications of a general shortage of child psychiatrists; and many of those who do treat children appear to be reluctant to treat visually handicapped children, perhaps because they believe that the psychiatric problems of the visually handicapped child are likely to be of a very different order from the psychiatric problems of the sighted child. Regular visits by psychiatrists to special schools for the visually handicapped are exceptional.

Evidence received

3.27 The survey by Dr Fine of visually handicapped children in special schools (already referred to) showed that 36% of the blind children and 32% of the partially sighted children were considered by their teachers to be emotionally disturbed. Although this was not a psychiatric assessment and there are no comparative figures for emotional disturbance in sighted children, Dr Fine concluded that this indicated a need for facilities for psychological and psychiatric investigation of these children. In our letter seeking evidence we asked specifically about the prevalence of emotional disorder among visually handicapped children and the extent to which psychiatric services should be made available to the special schools. There was a wide range of estimates of the prevalence of emotional disorder. In part of a study by R. G. Lansdown, J. Kell and D. Milner in 1970 of 100 children between the ages of 7 and 12 in three schools for the partially sighted in London, the Rutter Scale was used by one of our members to give a measure of social adjustment; this part of the study was later extended to children in the same age group at Exhall Grange. The sample suggested that these schools did not have an undue proportion of disturbed children as compared with Rutter's estimate of the normal prevalence. The Federation of the Blind in the UK, together with the head masters of 2 or 3 schools for the visually handicapped, thought that there was no significant difference between visually handicapped and normal children in the prevalence of emotional disturbance. The great majority, however, of those replying on this point considered that the prevalence of emotional disturbance among visually handicapped children is high, as Dr Fine's survey had suggested. Indeed more of those submitting evidence were agreed about this than on any other single issue raised in any of the evidence we received regarding medical services. Studies carried out in the United States indicated no personality differences between visually handicapped and sighted children.

3.28 There was less widespread agreement in the opinions expressed about the origins of emotional disturbance among the visually handicapped. Some regarded emotional disturbance as in some way inherent in the nature of the handicap; some thought that the disturbance arose only as a result of environmental circumstances and frustrations—such as over-protection or deprivation at home—which were more likely to be experienced by the visually handicapped child than the sighted, but would encourage emotional disturbance in any child whether handicapped or not; others again thought that much emotional disturbance could be ascribed to a child's anxiety as his visual acuity deteriorated over a period of time. Although these are opinions which lack supporting evidence, there appeared to be general agreement that psychiatric services for the visually handicapped needed substantial improvement.

Consideration of the issues

3.29 We are seriously concerned by the evidence that the prevalence of emotional disturbance among visually handicapped children may be high; and it seems to us vital that adequate facilities for the diagnosis and treatment of children and for the guidance of staff should be provided. If emotional disorders are recognised early and speedily treated, more intractable difficulties may be prevented from developing. Every school for blind and for partially sighted children needs to have regular links with a child guidance service or access to a consultant psychiatrist. A specialised psychiatric service for visually handicapped children is not required, but it would be advantageous if a larger number of psychiatrists and educational psychologists acquired expertise in dealing with these children. A detailed and systematic investigation is required of the extent, nature and causes of emotional maladjustment in visually handicapped children (see Chapter 10).

GENERAL MEDICAL CARE

3.30 We neither invited nor received evidence specifically on this subject but we think that a chapter on medical services would be seriously incomplete if nothing were said about it. As well as regular review by an assessment team, general medical supervision of visually handicapped children throughout pre-school and school years is important.

The present position

3.31 At present the nature of the provision varies according to the type of school. Day schools maintained by LEAs receive visits at varying intervals from local authority school medical officers, who also undertake school medical care of children in maintained boarding schools. All children resident in boarding schools, even on a weekly basis, are registered with a general medical practitioner for family doctor care including treatment of illness and prescription of drugs. It is not part of the contractual obligations of the general practitioner under the National Health Service to see children on admission to boarding school or for general medical supervision. Accordingly, such work in the non-maintained boarding schools may be carried out through private arrangements, the general practitioner receiving an honorarium from the school, as does an ophthalmologist providing regular supervision outside the hospital service. Many schools also have available a range of other specialists.

Consideration of the issues

3.32 There are good reasons why visually handicapped children should be medically examined more frequently than healthy children in ordinary schools. The effect of a specific handicap on general health and well-being must be observed and the presence of other handicaps ascertained. The increasing prevalence of multiple handicap, which we have noted in the two preceding chapters, underlines the importance of medical observation and treatment of any minor handicaps which are present. Routine prophylactic immunization procedures should be made available at the appropriate times. Hearing is particularly important for visually handicapped children, and audiometric sweep tests should be carried out on school entrants and subsequently as required. Visually handicapped children need to have an annual medical review which includes observation of the child in the classroom and at play. Advice should be offered to the parents and teachers on the implications of the handicap and the needs of the child. The need in a large number of cases for speech therapy, physiotherapy or orthopaedic or other treatment should be borne in mind and steps taken to supply the appropriate treatment. All routine medical services for children in special schools for the visually handicapped, including non-maintained schools, should in our view be carried out by the school health service.

3.33 As with other children, it is better that a few visually handicapped children should be seen thoroughly by the school doctor each week or fortnight and discussion take place with the head teacher and class teacher about any current problems, than that he should make a series of concentrated visits early in the term or year and there should then be a long interval before he comes again. More frequent inspection of all children should be carried out by the school nurse or welfare staff, who should bring any child causing concern to the attention of the school doctor. The school doctor and nurse will need to check, when dealing with visually handicapped children not in special schools for these children, that all concerned are aware of the child's needs in the classroom for a suitable desk, lighting etc., that he is using any visual aids which will help him and that he has been recently seen by the ophthalmologist. Other normal responsibilities of the school medical officer include suitability and hygiene of the school premises, particularly of the sick bay in boarding schools, and assurance that the standards of child care and the quality of school meals are high.

3.34 There are a few visual defects which are often accompanied by special dental problems. It is therefore particularly important that general dental care, with regular termly inspection and treatment of diseased or abnormal teeth, should be made available to all visually handicapped children in day and boarding schools through the local authority school dental service or from general dental practitioners. Some parents may, however, prefer to arrange for any necessary treatment to be carried out during school holidays. Particular attention should be paid by their dentists to children whose visual handicap is associated with specific dental problems.

3.35 Local education authorities should receive follow-up medical and educational reports on children sent to schools in other areas. Good communication is essential between the medical services concerned with visually handicapped children at boarding school and at home in the holidays, so that both are aware of any change in a child's condition or of any medical advice or treatment given.

RECOMMENDATIONS

3.36 We recommend that:

(1) all children should be screened for visual handicap at child health clinics as part of a general developmental assessment (paragraph 3.08);

(2) children identified as possibly having a visual abnormality should be referred for examination and treatment to the local ophthalmologist who would be a member of a comprehensive district assessment team. Children should receive a paediatric examination from this team, the key members of which should be a paediatrician, an ophthalmologist, a local authority medical officer and, when he could participate, the child's general practitioner, together with an otologist, a health visitor, a social worker, and other experts as required (paragraph 3.08);

(3) visually handicapped children should then be referred for combined ophthalmological/educational assessment to a regional assessment team including an ophthalmologist with particular skill and an interest in children, an educational psychologist and a teacher of the visually handicapped (paragraph 3.09);

(4) wherever possible, the regional assessment team should examine the visually handicapped child in a school setting (paragraph 3.09);

(5) all visually handicapped children should be regularly re-assessed (paragraph 3.10);

(6) parents should be kept informed about their child's condition and the help he needs (paragraph 3.11);

(7) a new form of notification of a visual handicap is required and a revised form of certification when a pupil leaves school (paragraph 3.12);

(8) vision screening of all children, including annual tests of visual acuity, should be part of school health services in all primary and secondary schools and special schools for other handicaps. The ophthalmic services for visually handicapped children attending these schools must be of the standard provided in a special school for the visually handicapped (paragraph 3.15);

(9) all schools for the visually handicapped should be visited regularly by a consultant ophthalmologist and an optician working for the National Health Service on a sessional basis, and should be equipped with a suitable examination room. There should be close co-operation between the ophthalmologist and the teaching staff, and between the optician and the ophthalmologist in the supply and maintenance of spectacles and low visual aids (paragraphs 3.18 and 3.19);

(10) genetic counselling should be made available to all parents and older visually handicapped children, through either the ophthalmologist in the regional assessment team or the ophthalmologist in each comprehensive assessment team based on a district general hospital (paragraphs 3.24 and 3.25);

(11) every school for the visually handicapped should have regular links with a child guidance service or access to a consultant psychiatrist (paragraph 3.29);

(12) visually handicapped children should receive a general medical examination more frequently than sighted children; and the school nurse or welfare staff should maintain continuous and close observation of the general health of all children in their care (paragraphs 3.32 and 3.33);

(13) the local authority school medical and dental services should be made available to all visually handicapped children in day or boarding schools (paragraphs 3.32 and 3.34); and

(14) local education authorities should receive follow-up medical and educational reports on children sent to schools in other areas; and there should be good communication between the medical services responsible for visually handicapped children at boarding school and in home areas (paragraph 3.35).

CHAPTER 4 : MEETING THE NEEDS OF CHILDREN UNDER 5

THE FIRST FIVE YEARS OF LIFE

4.01 The first five years are a period of very rapid development, intellectual and emotional as well as physical. In these years children acquire control of their bodies, they learn to play and talk and understand their physical environment, and they establish their first relationships with parents and peers. When a child is born with a physical or mental defect or acquires one early in life, his development may be impeded in a number of ways. From comparative studies of sighted and blind children there is evidence that the average young blind child—and to a lesser extent the partially sighted child—progresses more slowly in environmental understanding, language and social and motor development than the fully sighted child. It was found by Gomulicki[1], for example, that the young blind child might be inferior to the sighted one in a number of non-visual skills, including the tactile perception of shape. Russian studies also have demonstrated poor differentiation in the young blind child's recognition of household objects, which tend to be given generic rather than specific names. Gomulicki suggested that normally a general integration of a wide variety of sensory data is carried out through the visual sense. It is almost impossible to carry out this integration through the operation of senses other than vision.

4.02 The way in which some of these difficulties arise is obvious but for others the explanation is more subtle. From a very early stage sight plays a vital role in attracting the child to activity and to an interest in people and things in the world around him. Unless sufficient stimulus is provided from other sources, a visually handicapped child will probably be late in learning to sit up, to crawl, to stand and to walk. Later on, many of these children in school suffer from poor posture or exhibit repetitive mannerisms; these often have their origin in lack of training in early life. The visually handicapped child needs to be given every opportunity and encouragement to explore the environment and to grasp its spatial characteristics. He also requires to learn how to manipulate objects and identify them through touch, hearing and the other senses. The development of language may be impaired because the fully sighted child grasps the meaning of many words by seeing the object or the action to which they refer. The visually handicapped child is less able to do this; he may acquire speech by imitation, but often his questions and his speech generally will reveal that he does not understand how the words he is using apply to the real environment.

4.03 Miss Eira Clarke, a former headteacher of a Sunshine Home School, made at the request of the Committee a survey of young blind children and her report contains some graphic illustrations of the effects of their handicap on development and learning. The beginning of all discovery of what the world and the

---

[1] Gomulicki, B. R.: The Development of Perception and Learning in Blind Children, Cambridge University, Psychological Laboratory, 1961.

objects in it were like was when a baby in his first year realised that if he saw something he could also reach out and touch it, that he could move it about and try to taste it. Later on, he might see a coloured ball lying near him and would stretch out to retrieve it; it might roll out of his reach; by continued efforts he discovered how to shuffle or crawl towards it. Then he learnt to pull himself up by hanging on to furniture and eventually he was walking. Totally blind children were deprived of most incentives to stimulate movement during their early months. This delay in mobility made considerable impact on the adaptive behaviour and language of congenitally blind children. A child might hear a cat say " miaow ", but until he had held it, stroked it and been told that it was a cat, and had been near to it while it made the sound the relationship of one to the other was not fully understood. Sense of distance also was affected, since blind children could not obtain a real idea of spatial orientation.

4.04 A visual handicap in a child was bound to cause anxiety in parents. This anxiety sometimes led to stress within the family which might affect a child's cognitive and emotional development. Parents were often shocked and depressed, and might even feel guilty, when they found that a child of theirs was visually handicapped. Sight also played a major part in the mother-child relationship. Parents might find it difficult to develop a satisfying interaction between themselves and a visually handicapped child. Any additional handicaps a child may have increase the parents' bewilderment.

4.05 Miss Clarke found that some parents at first thought it inevitable that blindness must preclude happiness. They identified themselves with their children, forgetting that these had never seen and in their early years were not aware of the significance of their deprivation. Parents needed to be given hope, not of a cure for their child's blindness but of the possibility of a rich and full life for him; and it was vital to convince the parents that they more than anybody else had it within their power to help their child towards this goal. For some parents it was extremely difficult, but others soon came to terms with their child's disability and showed a natural capacity to bring him up effectively. Time, patience and a positive attitude to what blind children could do were the prime needs of parents—and teachers—in training them. The mother of a blind child needed to acquire the art of talking to him about what he was doing, what she was doing and what was happening round about. She should give him opportunities to handle a variety of objects, toys, utensils etc., describing them and naming them as he did so. The everyday activities of the mother—cleaning, cooking and shopping—were the very foundations on which a blind child's future knowledge was built, if she could use them with imagination and give the child time and opportunity to involve himself with all that she was doing.

4.06 It is encouraging that Gomulicki found that after the age of 5 some blind children were able to perform many tasks as well as sighted children. The parents of these blind children had not restricted or over-protected them, but had encouraged them to be active and independent, and had provided them with wide opportunities for developing the effective use of senses other than vision. An extensive American study by Norris, Spaulding and Brodie[2] also indicated

---

[2] Norris, M., Spaulding, P. J. and Brodie, F. H.; Blindness in Children, University of Chicago Press, 1957.

that overall development need not be slower in the blind child, provided that he has favourable opportunities for learning in the pre-school period based on the security and understanding supplied by the family. In the absence of these conditions, there may be permanent and irremediable damage both to intellectual functioning and also to emotional stability.

4.07 The needs of partially sighted children and of blind children with good residual vision in the early years are in some ways identical with those of the totally blind. Since however these children are able to develop concepts based on visual experience, they will not suffer from the effects of complete deprivation, which without skilled help can leave significant gaps in the cognitive development of the totally blind. There is, nevertheless, a real danger of confusion and inaccuracy arising in the conceptual and cognitive development of the partially sighted. The condition of partial sight is subject to a wide range of individual variations and it is not always possible for parents to form an adequate picture of the child's visual capacity. The child without perfect vision cannot know what he is failing to see in a given situation; he may give an apparently satisfactory impression of comprehension when he is in fact comprehending imperfectly or, in a complex situation, misunderstanding completely. It is for this reason that young partially sighted children may become excessively timid in strange surroundings since they have learned to mistrust their faulty grasp of the situation. Conversely, it is easy for a partially sighted child's visual capacity to be underestimated and for parents to be reluctant to allow a full and natural exploration of the child's surroundings. In these circumstances children may exhibit signs of frustration and behave in a bizarre fashion in an unconscious attempt to draw attention to their needs. Those concerned with young partially sighted children should be prepared to carry out a subtle and carefully timed running commentary on aspects of everyday activities where details are likely to be masked by imperfect vision, to elucidate and explain where necessary and above all to encourage the child to participate as fully as possible in all that is going on around him.

THE COUNSELLING OF PARENTS

The present position

4.08 For the parents of young visually handicapped children, there are two main sources of advice and support from local authorities—health visitors employed by health departments and social workers employed by social services departments. Health visitors are state registered nurses with some midwifery training who receive an extra year of training in health visiting. They work on an area basis and provide a counselling service to mothers on the healthy development of young children. As mentioned in the previous chapter, the health visitor may be one of the first people to identify a child as possibly suffering from a visual handicap. In the same way as health visitors are concerned with health care, so the social workers are concerned with the social and emotional aspects of human growth and development, and they are trained to help individuals and families with personal problems. They too work on an area basis; and they can call on colleagues with knowledge of the special aspects of blindness (or other handicapping conditions) as required.

4.09 There are at present two kinds of training designed to equip staff in social services departments to meet the special needs of blind people:

(a) a 3-months' course for qualified social workers which leads to the certificate in social work with the blind. These social workers will have an understanding of the individual needs of the blind child and his family, the special services available to them, and the knowledge of how social work methods and skills may be adapted to work with blind people;

(b) a 1-year course for unqualified staff leading to the certificate for social welfare officers for the blind. The training is designed to equip staff to help blind people to live without sight, teaching them such things as methods of communication, aids to living and recreational activities. These social welfare officers work mainly with blind adults, and their experience in helping relatives of newly blind people can be of great importance.

4.10 There have been a few developments in providing counselling by teachers and other staff associated with special schools. The school at Bridgend has appointed a full-time social worker, who is concerned with children due to enter as well as those already in the school. The Birmingham Royal Institution for the Blind has since January 1970 provided for an experimental 3-year period an experienced teacher of the blind, formerly the head of a Sunshine Home school, to undertake pre-school counselling. It was intended that she should work primarily in the West Midlands, but in fact the demand for her services has been much wider. Many of the children that she has visited are not suitable for schools for the blind, and their families are in particular need of supportive services. In addition to visiting carried out by the heads and senior staff of Sunshine Home schools, the RNIB maintains a parents' unit, transferred to Northwood (Middlesex) in 1964, where mothers (and when possible fathers) stay for 4–6 days with their children, who are usually 2 or 3 years old at the time. About 15 families a year stay at the unit. It too is at present run by the former head of a Sunshine Home school, who undertakes home visiting. Parents have an opportunity in a relaxed atmosphere to talk over the wide range of problems which are encountered in rearing a blind child. Nearby is the Northwood Sunshine Home school, where parents can see for themselves how blind children learn at the nursery stage. The general experience of all the staff involved is that it is the home visits which are of the greatest value. There are however insufficient staff available to make the visits soon enough after the initial request or with sufficient frequency where follow-up is required. As a further service, the RNIB issues a range of publications for the guidance of parents of blind children.

4.11 Social workers employed by local authorities may also visit partially sighted children. There is no special training for work with the partially sighted and their families, though there is a growing recognition of their needs in the present training courses for work with the blind described in paragraph 4.09. There are also hardly any formal arrangements for pre-school counselling of an educational nature. Some of the special schools, however, which cater for partially sighted children are able to give advice to parents of children whose

25

C

presence is notified to them. Exhall Grange School sends out to parents a leaflet which we have seen and think deserves a wider distribution.[3]

Evidence received

4.12 Miss Clarke reported that, from statements by parents of children at Sunshine Home schools and other schools for the blind, it appeared that many felt they had not had the early support and help they needed. Many also expressed the wish that they could have known of the welfare and educational facilities for their children at an early stage in their infancy. A number would like to have been put in touch with parents of other blind children, whilst several would have liked to have had earlier contact with the school prior to admission. Some parents wished they had had the opportunity to learn braille before the children went to school.

4.13 A survey[4], conducted by Dr. J. N. Langdon in 1966–68 in 7 Midland counties of about 10% of the national total of young people registered as blind showed that, out of 137 cases, the parents of 73 complained about the absence or inadequacy of counselling at or immediately after diagnosis; but once contact had been made with the blind welfare service, the parents of only 18 children expressed dissatisfaction whereas the parents of 96 were positively satisfied. A subsequent report[5] published in 1971 by Dr Langdon said that recent figures showed a slight reduction in the incidence of complaints by parents of young blind children, but 31% complained about the lack of non-medical counselling.

4.14 Another survey was made by two of our members who investigated the provision for partially sighted children and their parents in 1969. The survey was based on questionnaires sent to parents of children at Exhall Grange and ILEA's day schools for partially sighted children, thus covering about 35% of partially sighted children of school age. About 70% of the Exhall Grange children and 30% of the London children had been visited at home; in each group nearly half had been visited by welfare officers for the blind and others by doctors or nurses. It was remarkable that, although only 2% of the Exhall Grange parents and 5% of the London parents said that they found the visits of positive help, about one third said that they would have welcomed more frequent visits. This underlines the psychological need for reassurance. At the same time, almost all the parents would welcome advice on day-to-day handling of their children as well as information on possible future placements. They would prefer to have this from people experienced in the special needs of the partially sighted, as their visitors were not.

4.15 The evidence we received showed widespread support for a comprehensive service of counselling, available to all parents of visually handicapped children and covering the three aspects mentioned in the last paragraph, ie psychological support, advice about the day-to-day management of children and information about future educational provision. There was a variety of views expressed about who the counsellors should be and how they should be organised, but the

---

[3] We understand that a series of pamphlets giving guidance to parents of partially sighted children is to be issued by the Society for the Visually Handicapped, and that the Exhall Grange leaflet will be included in it.

[4] New Beacon: 1968—Vol. 52 No. 619 and 1969—Vol. 53 No. 622.

[5] New Beacon: 1971—Vol. 55, No. 650.

commonest opinion was that they should be based on special schools for the blind and the partially sighted, including the Sunshine Home schools. Health visitors and social workers had their supporters and their critics: it was for example pointed out by several witnesses that social welfare officers for the blind were primarily trained to meet the needs of adults and already had heavy case-loads. A team approach was favoured by a few: the RNIB, for instance, envisaged that " each (regional) team would consist of at least one member whose experience/training lay mainly in the field of child development and social work; and one member whose experience/training was in teaching and included some experience of teaching young blind children." The teams would not be attached to schools but " would work in closest association with all appropriate statutory and voluntary agencies." Attention was also drawn in some evidence to the importance, as counterpart to home visiting, of parents being able to visit schools and, if possible, to stay at them.

4.16 The evidence available about the practice in other countries suggests that the counselling of parents of visually handicapped children is generally unsatisfactory or at least patchy. An exception is Denmark where there is early identification and a counselling service operates with teachers visiting homes and Kindergartens. In some areas of the USA there is a full-scale service which includes training courses for parents, which are also run with success for parents of blind children in West Germany.

Consideration of the issues

4.17 It is evident that the need for a service capable of carrying out comprehensive counselling is urgent and is not satisfactorily met at present. The first two aspects of counselling already mentioned—psychological support and advice about the day-to-day handling of children—seem to us to call for staff with specialised knowledge of both blindness and partial sight, in children and not in adults, and with training or relevant experience in social work. We recommend that every local authority should be responsible for securing an adequate number of staff with the requisite training and knowledge who should act as counsellors to the parents of visually handicapped children in the authority's area. These counsellors would work in association with the regional assessment team described in the previous chapter. They should begin visiting the parents as soon as a child has been identified as having a visual handicap; until then health visitors could provide the parents with general support.

4.18 The third aspect of counselling—information about educational provision and also ways of promoting general cognitive development—is equally essential. It should be carried out by somebody trained as a teacher or an educational psychologist. One possibility would be the peripatetic teacher for the area (see paragraph 4.35); he would work in close association with the counsellors and with the regional assessment team, which should co-ordinate their work. Experience has shown that the different aspects of counselling tend to overlap and that distinct duties cannot always be assigned to specific staff. What is important is that every family of a visually handicapped child should have access to a team of qualified and experienced workers who can meet its various needs; and that the workers themselves should feel that they are part of a regional and not a local service.

EDUCATIONAL AND DAY CARE PROVISION

4.19 Under this heading we include for convenience play groups and day nurseries as well as peripatetic teaching services, day nursery schools and units, and residential nursery schools.

The present position

4.20 The 6 Sunshine Home schools run by the RNIB constitute the main form of educational provision for young blind children at present. They are residential schools, situated at Northwood, East Grinstead, Leamington Spa, Wellington (Shropshire), Southport and Southerndown (Glamorgan); and in 1971 the total number of children at them was 90; with an age range from 3 to 9. The present chief function of the Sunshine Home schools is the assessment, care and training of children who are unsuitable at this age—and perhaps at any age—for normal schools for the blind and/or whose families cannot cope with the exceptional strains which their disabilities impose. Most of the children had one or more additional handicaps; the two most common were educational subnormality and cerebral palsy. As the need and potential of the children become clearer, parents and LEAs are advised on the possibilities for future placement. The Hampstead Child Therapy Clinic also runs a small day nursery school for young blind children.

4.21 The schools for the blind and the partially sighted do not generally admit children under the age of 5. In January 1971 there were only 5 blind and 20 partially sighted children under 5 in special schools for the visually handicapped. Most of these were 4 years old and may have been admitted the term before their fifth birthday. Since the young partially sighted children have no equivalent to the Sunshine Home schools for the blind, this means that there is no specialised provision for them. A number however attend ordinary nursery schools and classes. In one nursery school in Aylesbury one quarter of the children are handicapped, including some who are partially sighted, and the headmistress has a specialist qualification in teaching the handicapped.

4.22 Experience in catering successfully for a mixed group of young handicapped children, including the visually handicapped, is provided by the Katharine Elliott School, Shrewsbury, which takes children aged 2-11; and by some ILEA nursery groups attached to day special schools, which take children with a variety of handicaps apart from deafness. A number of young visually handicapped children with other handicaps is found in a variety of establishments. For example, some are in special schools for the physically handicapped and the delicate. Special schools and hospitals for the severely mentally handicapped also contain some young children with visual handicaps.

4.23 The value of a peripatetic teaching service has been shown with deaf and partially hearing children, but visual handicap is much less common than hearing loss. The low prevalence of visually handicapped children is probably the chief reason why only one LEA at present is known to employ a peripatetic teacher for visually handicapped children at home.

28

4.24 Some visually handicapped children are in day nurseries but the number is not known. Local authorities are encouraged to accept handicapped children and a few day nurseries provide exclusively for handicapped children. Other day nurseries accept a small number of handicapped children, either in a separate unit or in the groups within the nursery.

4.25 The pre-school play-group movement has developed rapidly in recent years. Some play-groups are arranged by local authorities in co-operation with parents, but the majority are formed by voluntary associations of parents with the aim of enriching the experience of their young children. In addition to providing care for a few hours each week, play-groups offer valuable support and help to mothers, and the opportunity to meet other mothers and to participate in local social activities. There are play-groups in some areas which have been set up specifically for handicapped children, but usually a small number of handicapped children is accepted into local play-groups. The Pre-school Play-groups Association has issued an appeal for specialist help with such children.

Evidence received

4.26 There was very wide agreement that to board young visually handicapped children away from home is undesirable except in very special circumstances. The Hampstead Child Therapy Clinic went so far as to express the view that " no blind child, however mature, needs even weekly boarding until he is 8 years old if the home is at all adequate." This general disapproval of boarding for young children did not imply criticism of the Sunshine Home schools, which were regarded by most witnesses as carrying out an extremely difficult task with considerable skill. Although some of them were too far from the children's homes and their premises were often not ideal for their present functions, the Homes had made considerable progress in recent years in admitting children with severe additional handicaps, in establishing the closest contact with parents and in running on the lines of family groups. It was agreed by many witnesses that there would be a continuing need for some residential places for blind children in circumstances very similar to those of the children at present found in the Sunshine Home schools, ie where children are multihandicapped and where parents, whether or not their children are very severely handicapped, cannot look after them satisfactorily at home. Whenever possible, weekly boarding was considered the desirable pattern. Residential establishments might also be useful for short stay purposes; for example, where there is a sudden domestic crisis, parents need a holiday or parents want advice on managing a blind child. No evidence was received that specialised residential provision was required for young partially sighted children.

4.27 The majority of witnesses favoured nursery education given in schools, units or groups to visually handicapped children while they were living at home. Three types of grouping received considerable support—in nursery schools for ordinary children, in mixed groups of handicapped children and in special units of visually handicapped children. We will summarise the evidence for each in turn.

(i) Nursery schools for ordinary children

4.28 Miss Clarke observed that the few blind children in her survey who were being educated in ordinary nursery and infant schools were receiving a wider and more liberal education than those in special schools for the blind. It was generally accepted that one school or nursery could cope with only one or two visually handicapped children, and then only in circumstances which were well expressed by Miss Clarke. At the end of her survey she recommended that " whenever possible blind children under 7 should be educated with sighted children in nursery and infant schools in the locality of their own homes." She laid down four conditions:

(a) the children must not be too severely handicapped physically, intellectually or emotionally;

(b) their homes must provide a secure environment;

(c) the LEA must appoint an additional member of staff to give special attention to the blind children and must provide any special equipment required; and

(d) the blind children's education must be supervised by experts in the field of the education of the blind.

4.29 A considerable number of parents who were covered by the survey conducted by two of our members (see paragraph 4.14) said they thought that their partially sighted children could have benefited from an ordinary nursery group. On the other hand, disadvantages were recognised. There would not be the specialised facilities available to a group of handicapped children. Where skilled supervision was not available, individual children might be over-protected by their sighted fellows and not be encouraged to develop independence. Generally speaking, however, the use of ordinary nursery schools was considered satisfactory for partially sighted children.

(ii) Mixed groups of handicapped children

4.30 The chief advantage claimed for this form of organisation was that a group could be established within reach of the children's homes in many areas where there were not sufficient visually handicapped children to make up a group and so to obtain the benefit of mixing with other children. Medical, teaching and child care staff also could be deployed to better advantage. One suggestion was that the totally deaf and the severely physically handicapped might have to be excluded from such a group.

(iii) Special units of visually handicapped children

4.31 The scatter of visually handicapped children meant that a viable unit of these children could be formed only in large urban areas, if the strain of daily travel was not to be excessive. Such units might suitably be attached to existing schools for the visually handicapped, as a very few were at present. It was generally considered that blind and partially sighted children could be taught together at this stage, though some headteachers of special schools for the partially sighted thought otherwise.

30

4.32 There was also support for a peripatetic teaching service, so long as sufficient well-qualified teachers could be appointed to give individual visually handicapped children the frequent, regular and skilled attention they need. A child on his own at home, however, visited by a single teacher, could not secure the enrichment of his life gained from contact with other children and adults. A peripatetic teaching service was thought to be of most value in rural areas where it was impracticable to form a group of handicapped children.

Consideration of the issues

4.33 We believe that some form of nursery education is of even greater importance for the visually handicapped than for the fully sighted child. The nursery school stage is invaluable for widening the experience of visually handicapped children and for ensuring that they receive the special guidance they need to promote their optimum mental and physical development. There should be complete flexibility for individual children about whether nursery education is full-time or part-time and about the age when it should start and stop. For many children the nursery approach should extend into the infant school stage.

4.34 We agree that children under 5 should not board away from home except in very special circumstances. So far as day facilities are concerned, it seems to us better that a visually handicapped child should participate in an educational group (eg a nursery school or class for ordinary children, a mixed group of handicapped children or a special unit of visually handicapped children) than that he should receive instruction by himself at home. If however for any reason a child cannot join an educational group, visits from a peripatetic teacher are essential; education received in this way might be combined with attendance at a day nursery or a play-group, if one is available and suitably staffed.

4.35 We should like to make a few points about the various kinds of educational provision:

(a) there is a serious shortage of nursery school places for all children and we recognise that other children besides the handicapped have a special need for admission. We realise too that a nursery school may be able to absorb only a very limited number of children with special difficulties. We hope however that, whenever possible, some priority can be given to visually handicapped children for whom places are sought. Appropriate staffing arrangements will be required on the lines suggested in paragraph 4.28.

(b) When the other handicaps are the major ones, children with multiple handicaps may best be placed in groups of young children in special schools catering for handicaps other than those of sight, so long as attention is paid to their visual defects.

(c) A peripatetic teaching service could not only provide pre-school education in certain circumstances for individual children but could also operate in conjunction with other forms of provision. We have already suggested in paragraph 4.18 that a peripatetic teacher, working in association with staff carrying out other forms of counselling and with the regional assessment team, might have particular responsibility for carrying out counselling about educational provision and ways of promoting cognitive development. Other possibilities are that a peripatetic teacher might supervise the induction and progress of a visually handicapped child going to an ordinary nursery school; or he might give advice and help to a play-group taking one or two visually handicapped children.

(d) We had some discussion about whether a peripatetic teacher should be based on a local education authority (even if he is serving a wider area) or on a special school for visually handicapped children. The chief argument for the teacher being based on a school is that it provides a concentration of valuable expertise to support him in his work; and many of the children he visits will enter the school in due course. The disadvantages are that parents tend to count on entry to that school for their child, and may feel aggrieved if the child is not accepted; and that the nearest school may be considerably further from a child's home than the offices of the local education authority. Moreover, children need help during school holidays as well as in term-time. Our conclusion is that, on balance, it is better that a peripatetic teaching service should be based on a local education authority. It is however important that LEA-based teachers should have regular contact with special schools for the visually handicapped in the area and should, as part of that contact, have meetings with the staff of schools.

4.36 It may be helpful if we set out some of the factors governing a decision on what is the best provision for a particular child. The strain involved in travel must be carefully weighed up. For children under 5 we think that an hour's travel time each way should be regarded as the absolute maximum, and less is desirable; suitable transport and escorts should be provided. The quality and attitude of staff also need to be assessed. In general, staff who are trained teachers should be able to offer children a richer and wider range of educative experiences than staff who are not. At the same time, understanding of, experience with and interest in handicapped children are important factors; so is the availability of expert help and advice for staff who are not accustomed to dealing with handicapped children.

4.37 Finally, we see a continuing need for some residential units for visually handicapped children, as suggested in the evidence we received, from which children should go home at week-ends whenever possible. The assumption by the education service of responsibility for the education of severely mentally handicapped children has widened the range of multi-handicapped blind children for whom residential places may be required. The RNIB themselves consider that the Sunshine Home schools require some physical reorganisation; and we shall return to the question of their distribution and management in Chapter 6.

RECOMMENDATIONS

4.38 We recommend that:

(1) every family of a visually handicapped child under the age of 5 should have access to a team who can meet their different needs for counselling.

32

To this end, local authorities should be responsible for securing an adequate number of staff with the requisite training and experience to provide, for parents of young visually handicapped children in their area, psychological support and advice about the day-to-day handling of their children. These staff should work in close association with the teachers or educational psychologists who would carry out educational counselling and with the regional assessment team, which should co-ordinate their work (paragraph 4.17 and 4.18);

(2) all visually handicapped children under 5 should at some stage receive some form of education, and a range of educational facilities should be available in each area, including a peripatetic teaching service (paragraphs 4.33 and 4.34); and

(3) children under 5 should not board away from home except in very special circumstances; and children in residential units should go home at week-ends whenever possible (paragraphs 4.34 and 4.37).

CHAPTER 5 : ORGANISATION OF SCHOOLS

INTRODUCTION

5.01 In considering the organisation of schools a number of questions arise. Should visually handicapped children live at home and attend school daily or should they go to boarding schools? Should they be educated with fully sighted children, with or without other handicaps? Should blind and partially sighted children be in the same school? Should boys and girls be educated together? Should there be variations of educational provision according to age, ability and additional handicaps?

5.02 We realised at the start that our conclusions on certain aspects might have implications for other aspects, for example in relation to the size of schools. We have taken into account throughout our basic premise that children should live at home if possible, or failing that should board as near home as practicable (see paragraphs 5.09–5.10), but otherwise we decided to consider each aspect on its merits in isolation and then at the end to look at the cumulative effect of the conclusions reached.

DAY ATTENDANCE OR BOARDING

The present position
5.03 In addition to the Sunshine Home schools for young blind children, which were considered in the previous chapter, there are 12 boarding special schools for blind children. There are no day special schools but in January 1971, 35 day pupils attended the boarding schools. For the partially sighted there are 5 boarding and 14 day special schools. There are also 2 boarding schools which cater for both blind and partially sighted children.

5.04 In many boarding schools, children are not merely allowed to go home at some week-ends but are encouraged to do so every week-end. This system is generally known as weekly boarding. The most common practice is for pupils to go home after afternoon school on Friday and to return in time for the morning session on Monday. Arrangements for travelling and payment for transport vary widely. The schools remain open at week-ends for children who do not go home and provide a programme of activities for them.

Evidence received
5.05 The general view was that, wherever possible, day education was preferable because, in the words of one witness, " it allows the child to remain a member of the family unit." As might be expected in a situation where the large majority of schools for the partially sighted are day schools, the evidence from these schools was more strongly in favour of day education than was the evidence from schools for the blind. It is however significant that several boarding schools for the blind

34

conceded that residential education had serious disadvantages. The headmaster of one school said that "the atmosphere of a boarding school is an artificial one and can never achieve the normality of a home background."

5.06 The main reason advanced why boarding provision was inevitable was that in many areas the number of children was insufficient to form a viable day school without requiring excessive travelling. Sometimes too, boarding was desirable because parents could not, for a variety of reasons, satisfactorily meet their children's needs. The more severe a child's handicap or handicaps, the more likely it was that boarding would be required. Where boarding had to be provided, there were gains as well as losses. In the words of the headmaster of a boarding school for the partially sighted, " many children, by going to a boarding school, have attained a self-reliance and an independence, and have found a companionship, that they may have missed at day school and home. A fuller programme of games and out-of-school activities is possible in a boarding school." The headmaster of a school for the blind stated that, " so far as multiply handicapped blind children are concerned, there are other benefits concerned with adequate medical supervision and treatment, adequate meaningful occupation, the training of social habits and skills etc." There was also the advantage of the longer day. The same headmaster said: " where the pace in class must not be too great and where many interruptions necessarily occur for treatments, a great number of interesting and educationally beneficial activities are carried on through clubs in the early evening."

5.07 Particular advantages in boarding for adolescent blind girls were seen by the staff of the selective school for girls, Chorleywood College. " At this stage the girls need to re-accept their blindness. By facing this handicap together . . . it is easier for them to adjust and they are therefore more likely to be balanced ultimately. Their future outlook with regard to career and marriage is easier if faced together . . . During adolescence all sorts of frictions and tensions arise, and children begin to get a new and different view of their parents. A sighted adolescent just gets out of the house till the tension has eased, but the blind girl, in particular, seems to get caught in it much more . . . Mothers tend to use their teen-age blind daughters too easily as a listening ear into which to pour their problems. Fathers are much too anxious about their safety to allow them reasonable freedom of movement."

5.08 Where boarding was necessary, weekly boarding at schools meeting regional needs was commonly advocated in order to preserve children's links with their home as much as possible. The maximum distance of home from school for reasonable regular contact was thought by several schools to be 75 miles. One school quoted with approbation the practice of a particular local education authority, in providing escorts for their children when returning home at week-ends. Support for weekly boarding was qualified in a few instances. The RNIB stated that they did not consider that weekly boarding was practicable for the schools they managed (which cater for children with special needs and, apart from the Sunshine Home schools, have a national catchment area), though they were anxious to continue to improve school-home links. Their selective school for boys, Worcester College, while not against weekly boarding in principle, pointed out that certain conditions were desirable:

(a) the school should not become geared to stopping entirely at **4 p.m.** on Fridays;

(b) the academic work—the first function of the school—should **not have** to take second place, and

(c) proper arrangements must be made for activities and pastoral care for those pupils who do remain at week-ends.

One or two witnesses claimed that frequent transition between the two worlds of home and school was unsettling for some children. Dr J. N. Langdon, formerly Principal of the Royal Normal College for the Blind, was in favour of weekly boarding at the primary, but not the secondary, stage.

Consideration of the issues

5.09 We believe that all blind and partially sighted children, except some of those with multiple handicaps or poor home conditions, could and should live at home if their home is within an hour's journey of a suitable school and provided their parents can be given guidance on child management. The exceptions cannot be stated more categorically because so much depends on the attitude of individual parents to their handicapped child and to boarding education for him, and on their ability to cope with him at home. Competent professional advice should be available to help parents to see what is in the best long-term interests of their child and, if boarding is indicated, to accept this without feeling it casts a slur either on their competence as parents or on their child's ability. This advice could appropriately be given by the peripatetic teacher for the area, working in association with the regional assessment team (see paragraphs 4.18 and 4.35). Where boarding education is decided on, it is most desirable that the parents and the child should visit the school well in advance of the time when he is due to go there.

5.10 Where day attendance is impracticable, weekly boarding seems to us the best way to maintain the links between children and their homes. It also makes it easier to recruit staff. We deal in the next chapter with the question of re-distributing boarding special schools for the visually handicapped on a regional basis; and it is sufficient to say here that weekly boarding will not be practicable unless the homes of children are within a maximum distance of somewhere between 50 and 75 miles. Local education authorities should pay travelling expenses or provide transport home at week-ends, and supply escorts if necessary. While certain modifications in the time-table are legitimate to facilitate weekly boarding, for example a shorter dinner hour on Fridays and a later timing than usual for the morning and afternoon sessions on Mondays, it is necessary that there should be two full sessions on each day if the regulations dealing with attendance at special schools are to be complied with. It is important that schools should provide adequately for the occupation and recreation of children who stay at boarding schools at week-ends.

5.11 The type of boarding accommodation required will vary according to children's age. Older boys and girls need to be prepared for leaving the protective atmosphere of a school and going out to a more independent life in the world. The separate sixth form block at Chorleywood provides one method of inculcating independence.

5.12 We also consider that all boarding schools should be prepared to accept children for boarding for short periods, where there is a domestic crisis or parents need a respite for other reasons.

EDUCATION IN ORDINARY SCHOOLS

5.13 The inclusion of some handicapped children in the ordinary classes of ordinary schools is often described as ' integrated education ' (sometimes as ' open education '). This description is usually applied to children living at home, but some children boarding away from home also obtain their education in ordinary classes of ordinary schools. Another possibility, which we consider as well, is to organise special classes of visually handicapped children as part of ordinary schools.

The present position

5.14 Only a very few blind children are known to have been placed in ordinary classes of ordinary schools while living at home. The number of partially sighted children so placed, who would generally be considered to require to attend a special school, is larger. The number in England is not known, but a recent survey conducted in Wales by HM Inspectors and one of the Department's Medical Officers revealed 78 partially sighted children in ordinary schools. No information was available about 18 of these; of the remaining 60, 34 were considered to be making satisfactory progress, 12 were on waiting lists for special schools and the parents of 14 had refused special school places for them.

5.15 At St. Vincent's School for the Blind and Partially Sighted, selected blind children have since 1961 been going daily to local grammar schools to take academic courses; they are assisted by an education counsellor and there are satisfactory arrangements for transcription of books into braille. Partially sighted children at St. Vincent's, however, who require academic courses are transferred to Exhall Grange. Since 1969 six selected pupils from Tapton Mount School, Sheffield, which takes blind children aged 5–12, have proceeded for secondary education to a nearby comprehensive school, while living in a hostel on the campus of Tapton Mount. Apart from the full-time schemes based on these two schools, in a few special schools for the blind and the partially sighted some of the older children are sent part-time to ordinary secondary schools or colleges of further education, e.g. for ' O ' and ' A ' level courses in certain subjects.

5.16 *Special Classes* No special classes for blind children exist, so far as is known. One reason presumably is that, when age-range is taken into account, there are not sufficient blind children in the area of any ordinary school to make up a satisfactory special class. In January, 1971 there were 9 special classes for partially sighted children attached to 8 ordinary schools, containing 86 children in all; 7 of the 9 classes catered for children of primary age.

Evidence received

5.17 The RNIB pointed out that " the main justification in favour of ' open education ' would appear to be on social rather than educational grounds, i.e.

integration with the sighted community and continuous contact with the family."
At the same time, the RNIB said: " We feel that ' open education ' has become
a dangerous catch-phrase, and parents will erroneously assume that any visually
handicapped child can be absorbed into a sighted school programme; and that
by going to a sighted school he will automatically make and keep sighted friends,
receive as good an education as he would get in a school for the visually handicapped, and become a fully integrated member of the community."

5.18 Of particular interest is the evidence received from visually handicapped
adults who had attended ordinary schools, or from the parents of visually handicapped children who attended such schools. These sources, as well as other
witnesses, differed about the merits of integrated education. One blind girl who
throve in an ordinary school had " high intelligence and tremendous zest for
work," as well as support from home. A partially sighted boy of 6, who also
was doing well in the local primary school, was described by his mother as
" a merry little boy, very outgoing and . . . with a good deal of common sense."
There were however difficulties at first: he sat at the back of the class and could
not see the blackboard; he was left behind by the other children when toys etc.
were distributed; and he was afraid of the steps. Another person, who described herself as partially sighted but later taught blind children, emphasised
the importance to a child " of being free of frustration and able to find his or her
own level in a class." She wrote of her own experience: " While at school with
normally sighted children this feeling of inferiority increased and became
painful. I was keen to learn but was frustrated; I loved organised games but
was debarred; while others were doing needlework I was given odd jobs; worst
of all I had to sit in front of the class right under the blackboard and then could
not see it properly."

5.19 A survey carried out by one of our members has thrown some light on the
factors which make for the success of integrated education for partially sighted
children. The 68 children between the ages of 4 and 18 covered by the survey
were referred from a variety of sources all over the country for advice and help.
Although the sample is thus not an unbiassed one, analysis showed that children
with intelligence above average and enlightened parental support were more
likely to flourish in ordinary schools. Other factors conducive to successful
placement were earlier attendance at a special school for the partially sighted
and careful selection; continuing support from a particular member of the staff
of the ordinary school; small classes; ready access to ophthalmic advice; and
regular reviews of placement.

5.20 Miss W. E. Deavin, formerly HM Inspector with special responsibility for
the education of the visually handicapped, summed up the position as follows:
". . . the majority of teachers do not know the special techniques, methods,
equipment etc. required in the education of children in all categories of handicap.
When experiments of this kind are made, especially in the case of blind children,
care must be taken to see that the conditions in the ordinary school are suitable
as far as premises, organisations etc. are concerned; that the school is one which
welcomes the exceptional child; that the staff involved are prepared to accept
help and advice. The child, too, must be carefully selected. It is most likely to
work with an intelligent, competent, independent child who has already learnt

self-management and the basic skills of reading and writing braille . . . Too many partially sighted children, however, have fallen sadly behind at their ordinary schools before being transferred to a special school. The lively, active visual methods which pertain in the average good primary school today may make it difficult for a severely visually handicapped child to fit into a large class of ordinary children."

5.21 Tapton Mount School supplied a detailed account of their scheme (mentioned in paragraph 5.15) for sending selected blind children for secondary education to a nearby comprehensive school, and the particulars in this paragraph and the next are taken from it. The first 4 children chosen were said not to be of outstanding ability, but to be emotionally mature and to have plenty of perseverance; they also had some residual sight. The 2 children who went to the comprehensive school in 1971 were " totally blind or near to it," but of much higher intelligence. The first children are now completely accepted at the school; they mix freely with the sighted children and have their own friends; their mobility and independence have all increased remarkably; their physical movements have become natural and easy; and each member of the group has become a much more lively individual. Two of the first group told their parents that they liked going to the comprehensive school because they no longer felt blind. In order to keep up with the work of the comprehensive school, the children have had to learn to work more quickly than before; to type their homework; to study tape-recorded material and to tape-record their own notes; and to carry out cross-referencing much more extensively, e.g. between tape-recorded material and braille books.

5.22 The school stated that the success of the scheme has owed much to the resource teacher on the staff of Tapton Mount, who in the early stages lived in the hostel. New techniques and equipment have reduced the need for blind children to carry around bulky braille books and braillers in a crowded school: at the comprehensive school all that the Tapton Mount children carry about is a very small, light tape-recorder. At the same time, the support services required to maintain a handful of children in the comprehensive school are of a truly formidable extent and complexity. Four groups (one of which consists of prisoners at Wakefield) and a large number of individuals transcribe into braille material which includes foreign languages and mathematics; members of a Rotary and an Inner Wheel club, two girl guides and a retired man help with thermoform duplicating; a speech therapist records texts on a cassette; the wife of a university registrar produces map outlines; and college of education students draw maps and text book diagrams (some sixth form school children help with this too), and make scientific and other apparatus.

5.23 In most European countries blind children are segregated for their education from sighted children. But in the USA a survey by Nolan and Ashcroft[1] indicated that 59% of over 20,000 children registered as blind were in sighted schools. (The different criteria for registration used in the United States result in a greater proportion of children than in this country being registered as blind). In general, special provision was made for them by means of ' resource

---

[1] Nolan, C. Y. and Ashcroft, S. C. The visually handicapped. Review of Educational Research XXXIX, No. 1, February 1969, pp 52–70.

rooms ' and/or itinerant teachers for teaching braille, etc., though the bulk of the teaching was undertaken by non-specialist teachers in ordinary classes. But the visual acuity of these children was in general greater than that of children in special schools for the blind (Jones[2]). Even totally blind children in sighted schools were found by McGuinness[3] not to be inferior to those in special schools when their braille reading was tested; and the former were superior to the latter in social maturity and social integration. However, another study by Havill[4] showed that the estimated sociometric status of blind children was inferior to that of their sighted classmates, and they were less well accepted; above average achievement improved the status of blind children. Lukoff and Whiteman[5] found that blind children in special schools showed a lower degree of independence than those in sighted schools. But those for whom family influences were unfavourable to the development of independence benefited most from special education.

5.24 Avery[6] has described the deficiencies in integrated education for the visually handicapped in the USA. He said that the needs of the sighted were considered first in sighted schools. The visually handicapped child might remain in the same grade year after year because he did not progress at the same rate as the sighted. Some teachers were too sympathetic to the visually handicapped, and had too low an expectation of his progress; thus they were satisfied with minimal performance. Other teachers had too high an expectation and were too critical of slowness in the visually handicapped. Library and musical facilities and physical activities for the visually handicapped were inadequate. Courses in mobility were seldom available and there was no specific training in acquiring daily living skills. The sighted and the visually handicapped did not mix easily, and the former did not like helping the latter. However, the older visually handicapped children profited more from integrated education than did the younger, because there was more social acceptance. A child and his parents might feel a loss of face if he did not do well in a sighted school and it was recommended that he should attend a special school. On the other hand, residential schools tended to be slow to relinquish to integrated education their more intelligent and socially acceptable children. Magleby and Farley[7] compared 59 visually handicapped adults educated in residential schools for the blind with 39 educated in sighted schools (all were handicapped before 3 years). Almost twice as many of the former were blind as of the latter; but the former had had a more prolonged period of education than the latter. More of the former could read braille and had received vocational training. Their social contacts were wider and their attitudes to life more positive.

[2] Jones, J. W. Blind children: degree of vision, mode of reading. Washington, U.S. Office of Education, Bulletin No. 26, 1961.
[3] McGuinness, R. M. A descriptive study of blind children educated in the itinerant teacher, resource room and special school settings. A.F.B. Research Bulletin No. 20, March 1970, pp. 1–56.
[4] Havill, S. J. The sociometric status of visually handicapped students in public school classes. A.F.B. Research Bulletin No. 20, March 1970, pp. 57–90.
[5] Lukoff, I. F. and Whiteman, M. Socialisation and segrated education. A.F.B. Research Bulletin No. 20, March 1970, pp. 91–107.
[6] Avery, C. D. A psychologist looks at the issue of public v residential school placement for the blind. New Outlook, 1968.
[7] Magleby, F. Le G. and Farley, O. W. Education for blind children. Research Bulletin No. 16, 1968.

5.25 *Special Classes* Less evidence was submitted on this aspect of the subject. In what was received attention was more widely drawn to the disadvantages of special classes for partially sighted children than to their advantages. One striking account of a special class that we received in the last months of our deliberations suggested that in certain circumstances the staff and children of the ordinary school may not accept the partially sighted and may treat them thoughtlessly and unkindly. Tobin[8] found that teachers of sighted children often knew little about the problems involved in teaching the visually handicapped and had no desire to teach them. The account also indicated that the special facilities needed by the partially sighted, including lighting, low visual aids and medical supervision, may not be provided; and staffing may be a problem. Again, one of the ILEA's special schools for the partially sighted stated roundly that " classes attached to ordinary schools hold the danger of the worst solution of all—isolation in a large community, which is far worse than the loneliness of the small community." At the same time, the school was not unequivocal in its condemnation: " Success is dependent on the degree to which ALL the staff involve themselves with the visually handicapped." Other conditions for success were that the children should not be too severely handicapped, visually or intellectually; and that the catchment area should be sufficiently large to avoid numbers sinking so low as to threaten viability. The Consultative Committee of the Head Teachers of the ILEA Schools was " not in favour of special classes in ordinary schools, as this often leads to emphasis on the handicap, and an attitude of restriction rather than encouragement to attempt new activities." It was also pointed out that a single class attached to a school might have to cater for too wide a range of age and ability.

5.26 Other witnesses have spoken of the advantages of special classes. The County Councils Association on balance " accept the general principle that wherever it is appropriate and practicable the visually handicapped child, and certainly the partially sighted child, should experience the fullest social contact with other children. The principle can best be satisfied by education in a special class or unit attached to an ordinary school." Again, it was remarked that a special class allows flexibility in the amount of time that partially sighted children spend with fully sighted children. Miss Deavin suggested that " a unit of several primary partially sighted classes attached to a good ordinary primary school has far better chances of success " than a single class.

5.27 One or two witnesses proposed that there should be special classes for blind children. One idea was that a special class with a small hostel attached would enable some blind children to live at home or at least to board at a much shorter distance from it than if, as at present, they had to attend a much larger residential school. A more elaborate scheme was put forward by the most whole-hearted advocate of integrated education among our witnesses. He was blind and had been educated in Glasgow in the 1930s, when all the blind children who were not Roman Catholics were educated in blind departments attached to two large ordinary schools. He was not in favour of simply including individual blind children in the nearest ordinary school, but he envisaged a system whereby blind departments were established in about 30 primary and

---

[8] M. J. Tobin. The attitudes of non-specialist teachers towards visually handicapped pupils. Teacher of the Blind, 1972, 60, No. 2.

41

30 related secondary schools in England and Wales. To begin with, young blind children would " receive all or most of their instruction in the blind departments but by the later stages of their primary education, and especially in the secondary schools, the blind children should receive by far the greater part of their education as members of the ordinary, predominantly sighted classes."

5.28 Overseas, the most common practice is for partially sighted children to be educated in special classes in ordinary schools. In Holland there are special schools for the partially sighted, both day and boarding.

5.29 In 1971 a report by Elizabeth M. Anderson was published under the title ' Making ordinary schools special ' on the integration of handicapped children in Scandinavian Schools, based on a visit in September, 1970 to Sweden, Norway and Denmark. All three countries are committed to a policy of integrated education, and special classes within ordinary schools are one of the forms of provision that are being extensively developed. Although the report concentrates on provision for the physically handicapped, mention was made of special classes for children suffering from other disabilities including those whose sight was impaired; and what was said about factors making for the success of special classes appeared to be of general application. The following were listed as pre-requisites for good staff relationships.

"(i) a head who was interested but not necessarily experienced in the education of the physically handicapped pupils;

 (ii) a common staff room;

(iii) a willingness on the part of the special staff to keep the ordinary teachers well informed about what they were doing;

(iv) a time-table and staffing ratio which allowed the special teachers to do some teaching in the ordinary classes and those of the ordinary staff, who were interested, some special class work."

The report continued: " It was suggested that when the ordinary children know the special teachers, and are also aware that their own teachers work in the special classes, they are more willing to accept the handicapped children on an equal basis. Both the amount of time which physically handicapped children spend with ordinary pupils and the quality of the interaction between them are important . . . one of the most useful pointers as to whether the child would fit in socially in the ordinary school appeared to be the extent to which he joined or was joined by children from the ordinary classes in the dining-room and playground."

Consideration of the issues

5.30 The current trend is to emphasise that handicapped children are above all children, with many needs that children without handicaps have too. This approach however has its dangers as well as its merits, since it can lead to a demand that handicapped children should be given exactly the same educational treatment as other children; and we realise that it is impossible for visually handicapped children to progress satisfactorily in a sighted school unless they are given special facilities. We recall however the importance which the Royal Commission of 1885 attached to blind children having ' free intercourse with

42

the seeing' (see paragraph 1.03); and we are deeply impressed by the argument that, if visually handicapped children are to be fitted through their education to live in the world with sighted people, the best way for them to acquire the necessary ability and confidence is to mix as freely as possible with sighted children during their schooldays. Social events arranged with neighbouring sighted schools may help a little, but contacts tend to be artificial or at least superficial; in order to get to know sighted children and to feel at home with them, a visually handicapped child needs to be in the same school as they are.

5.31 Comparatively little experience has been gained in this country of educating visually handicapped children in ordinary schools. Before any firm judgments can be made about the extent to which integrated education is possible for these children, we believe that further systematic experimentation, with education both in ordinary and in special classes, is desirable within the context of the national plan which we recommend in Chapter 6 should be drawn up. Some doubts have been cast on the whole concept of a special class by the failure of some of the existing ones for partially sighted children to achieve full integration with their parent school, but we are ready to believe that it is not the concept which is to blame but rather the human and material factors operating in individual cases. We hope that the Scandinavian experience with special classes will be found relevant to classes in this country. Moreover, it is difficult to see what other form of day provision would constitute a realistic alternative to special classes in an area where there are 20–30 partially sighted children of all ages and no special schools for other handicaps which might be suitable for them.

5.32 Further experiments with integrated education should test the validity of fears expressed on various counts, for example about the services likely to be available for technical and medical support. The Tapton Mount scheme demonstrates that, even for 6 children, technical supporting services are at present required which are far in excess of those normally available or necessary in schools for the blind. If a prohibitive amount of voluntary help is not to be called for, the amount of brailling required will have to be reduced (as Tapton Mount have now discovered ways of doing—see also Chapter 7) and arrangements will have to be made for a single set of support services to serve a large number of children. For the partially sighted too, facilities are needed for producing typed lesson notes and clear maps and diagrams and for recording books and materials on tapes. On the medical side, there are serious risks that the specialised care of visually handicapped children may fall short of the high standards desirable. The distance separating the ordinary school from the special regional assessment centre may be considerable. As a result there may be little expert supervision of spectacles or low visual aids; and, with probably only one resource teacher and little medical assistance, continued visual assessment may be poor. Another fear, where blind children live during the week in a school for the blind (or a hostel attached) is that some of them may be unsettled by dividing their time between three environments—an ordinary school, a school for the blind and their home at week-ends.

5.33 Particular care should be taken to ensure that the specialised medical and ophthalmological supervision reaches the same standard as that found in special schools for the visually handicapped. Besides adequate support services, vital factors in the success of a scheme of integration appear to be that:

43

(a) the children should be of stable personality and of at least average intelligence;

(b) regular reviews should be undertaken at each stage of their education to ensure that adequate progress is being made;

(c) their parents should support the scheme;

(d) the ordinary school should not merely welcome the children but the staff should be ready to take time and trouble to integrate them—and specialists in the education of the visually handicapped should be responsible for giving advice and support;

(e) special equipment should be provided on a generous scale, including for the partially sighted suitable lighting and low visual aids; and

(f) special arrangements should be made for mobility training and physical education.

In addition, for special classes three further points need to be emphasised:

(g) there should preferably not be more than two age-groups in a class, though family grouping can work well where the required teaching skills are available;

(h) the staff of the school must be prepared for visually handicapped children to work alongside sighted children for certain subjects and activities; and

(i) the staffing of the school must be sufficiently generous to enable the classes in which visually handicapped children are working to be smaller than their counterparts.

EDUCATION WITH CHILDREN SUFFERING FROM DIFFERENT HANDICAPS

The present position

5.34 Nine special schools primarily for the delicate or physically handicapped take some partially sighted children. The East Anglian School, Gorleston-on-Sea, caters for partially sighted and deaf children in separate departments. Exhall Grange School contains a number of physically handicapped children, of whom 90% are also partially sighted. There are 3 special school campuses which include a special school for partially sighted children—two in Birmingham and one in London.

Evidence received

5.35 Evidence on this question was not specifically invited, but views on it reached the Committee from six sources. All except one were in favour of educating visually handicapped children in the same schools as children suffering from other handicaps—though not necessarily all other handicaps or at all ages. The head of one school for the partially sighted suggested day nursery schools for children of different handicaps, though " it may be necessary to exclude the totally deaf, severely physically handicapped and, perhaps less necessarily, the totally blind." Miss Deavin (see paragraph 5.20) expressed the opinion that " a partially sighted unit attached to a school for delicate or physically handicapped children is NOT a good idea. The unit is generally too small and the partially sighted children tend to be treated as though they were delicate and the pace becomes very slow."

Consideration of the issues

5.36 We have discussed at some length a broader scheme of school organisation into which schools for the visually handicapped might fit. Experience at Exhall Grange and some of the special schools primarily for delicate or physically handicapped children has shown the advantages which some of us think lie in mixing groups of children suffering from different handicaps, provided the staff take the trouble to become knowledgeable about these. An alternative way of mixing children, which is more suited to a regional pattern of special school provision, would be to have several schools and units for different handicaps and combinations of handicaps on one or two campus sites near centres of population with good communications, sharing medical services and certain educational facilities and ancillary services. One or two ordinary primary and secondary schools should be near at hand. Others of us have considerable mis-givings about assembling large crowds of handicapped children and about putting children suffering from certain handicaps in close proximity, even if they are not in the same school, for example, the blind, the severely physically handicapped and the maladjusted. It would, of course, mean that in most areas the schools would have to be residential, but taking day pupils. So far too, the sharing of facilities on the existing campuses is said to have fallen short of expectations.

5.37 It would be a pity if the whole idea of a variety of schools on a campus site was rejected because of the inability or unwillingness of some special schools on existing campuses to work closely together. It may be that schools have not realised the benefits of co-operation in terms of enjoying teaching, medical and physical resources that would be beyond the reach of one school on its own; or the possibility of combining co-operation with a high degree of autonomy. We commend the idea that a committee of teachers should be set up representing all the schools involved, which would have responsibility for the use of the resources of the campus and would help to create a greater understanding of the needs of children with different handicaps. We all agree that one or two experiments on campus lines would be of great interest as and when it becomes possible to concentrate on one site some of the special schools to serve a region. We return to the question of regional planning in Chapter 6.

EDUCATION OF THE BLIND AND PARTIALLY SIGHTED IN THE SAME OR SEPARATE SCHOOLS

The present position

5.38 The 1934 Report of the Committee of Enquiry into problems relating to partially sighted children (see paragraph 1.05) recommended that the partially sighted should not, as a general rule, be sent to schools for the blind. There are now only 2 special schools, both all-age, where blind and partially sighted are educated in the same school—the School for Visually Handicapped Children, Bridgend, Glamorgan and St. Vincent's School for Blind and Partially Sighted,

Liverpool. In both cases there were special reasons for retaining provision for both groups, the school at Bridgend being the only provision for visually handicapped children in Wales and the school at Liverpool the only school for Roman Catholic children. Viable schools would have been impossible if an attempt had been made to cater for Welsh and RC blind and partially sighted children separately.

Evidence received

5.39 The experience of Bridgend and St. Vincent's Schools has been that the two degrees of visual handicap can be successfully accommodated in one school. Both too have reached the conclusion that blind and partially sighted children can be mixed in the same class in the early and late parts of their school career. Bridgend say that " the strongest argument for the separation of braille and print users has always probably referred to pupils in the early stages of learning braille and to slow-learning braille users;" but they are inclined to the view that " suitable braille-using children can be integrated in groups using print at any stage." St. Vincent's followed a policy of almost complete segregation, except out of school, for about 20 years up to 1968, but now children under 8 and from 14 onwards are placed in mixed classes.

5.40 An argument in favour of educating the blind and partially sighted together in one school was that it would enable more blind children to attend schools daily. Another was that it would be more economical for educational and medical services. The other main arguments were set out by St. Vincent's as follows:

(i) it is difficult to assess the educational efficacy of children's vision when they are young, except in an educational environment. In consequence, many children are wrongly placed: of a group of 13 children under the age of 8 admitted between 1966 and 1969, in at least 6 cases the initial recommendation for education as partially sighted or as educationally blind proved incorrect. Children wrongly placed in a school catering for the partially sighted or blind only may be left to struggle with an inappropriate medium beyond the stage of readiness to read; or they may be faced with the emotional upheaval of a change of school.

(ii) " The line of demarcation between the educationally blind and the partially sighted is becoming blurred, especially in the middle ranges of vision, i.e. 3/60–6/60. With the increasing efficiency of visual aids and lighting, and with the general improvement of print and lay-out in school books, it is possible for a child with low visual acuity to use sighted methods in one situation, e.g. mathematics, while making better progress with tactile methods in another, e.g. continuous reading. This situation is easier to cope with in a school where both methods are available."

(iii) " Some pupils with low vision manage quite well to pursue their studies by visual methods at close range but, when required later to work at arm's length, need to rely on tactile methods. This can be prepared for in a school where both teachers and equipment are readily available for the supplementary training."

5.41 The General Secretary of the Catholic Blind Institute and several other witnesses made the further point that a school covering the whole range of visual handicap would obviate the need for children to transfer to another school when their optical condition changed. It was also claimed that at St. Vincent's School the blind are stimulated to make wider use of any residual vision they have, e.g. in art lessons and physical activities.

5.42 Some witnesses firmly rejected combined schools, sometimes without giving reasons, though they usually added that they favoured closer liaison between schools for the blind and for the partially sighted and easy arrangements for transfer. Even witnesses who were on balance in favour of combined schools saw certain disadvantages in them. The fear was expressed that the special needs of the partially sighted children, particularly encouragement to make the fullest use of their vision, might be overlooked. It was also suggested that some parents would resent the idea of their children mixing with blind children: " the fact that their children are partially sighted and not blind (a much more emotively charged word) is one of the comforts of their situation." The fear was expressed that the blind would be over-protected by the partially sighted and lose their independence for mobility. Another comment was that the totally blind can become even more isolated, since the educationally blind children with some vision tend to play with the partially sighted.

Consideration of the issues

5.43 We all agree that the blind and the partially sighted each have some special needs. In acquiring their skills of reading and writing, and in compensating for the different degrees of visual handicap, the approach to learning is different for the two groups. The learning of mobility for blind and for partially sighted children is based on a different variety of experiences: for the blind, early training in tactile exploration is essential; for the partially sighted, insistence on the maximum use of vision at the earliest moment is equally vital. At this learning stage, direct association in the same classes may restrict the independence of each group.

5.44 If the special needs of the blind and the partially sighted, at the time when they are acquiring different skills for reading, writing and mobility, could be met in a combined school with two departments, we all agree that there would be substantial advantages in educating the two groups together. We are particularly impressed by the scope that would be created for keeping blind children nearer home (with some of them able to attend schools as day pupils) and for dealing flexibly with children who are on the borderline between educational blindness and partial sight or who need to employ visual and tactile methods for different kinds of work. Further, the larger numbers resulting should make it possible to provide better facilities, e.g. specialist teaching and classrooms, swimming pools, medical rooms and administrative and technical resources. Teachers trained through the Birmingham University course (see paragraph 9.03) to teach both blind and partially sighted children will be particularly valuable in combined schools.

5.45 Two of our members, however, part company from the majority of us in their attitude to the question whether the special needs of the two groups can in fact be met in the same schools; their views will be set out in the next paragraph. Two other members expressed no opinion on the subject. The majority of the committee believed that the blind and partially sighted will benefit from sharing classes at the infant and secondary stages, and consider that, even if the two groups require to be educated in separate classes at the junior stage, they will still gain at this period from forming part of the same school and mixing for certain communal activities. The majority therefore conclude that it is both possible and desirable that blind and partially sighted children should be educated in the same schools.

5.46 The two members[9] would have no hesitation in accepting the siting of schools or units for the blind and partially sighted along with those providing for children in other categories of handicap, and for children without handicaps, on the campus system (see paragraphs 5.36 and 5.37), thus securing the advantage of optimum facilities and specialist teaching for all. They would also welcome experiments, based on a shared home room system, for both the blind and the partially sighted in ordinary schools provided that full supporting services could be guaranteed (see paragraphs 5.31—5.33). Since, however, they consider the handicaps of blindness and partial sight to be different and distinct as outlined in paragraph 5.43, they would view the reorganisation into combined schools as a retrograde step which would militate against the interests of each category in the fields of research, mobility, involvement in the community and above all learning experience. They are convinced that the number of children in the borderline category is small; and they consider that the needs of the blind with good residual vision and the severely partially sighted can be met by imaginative treatment within each category and closer co-operation between schools within the same region or on the same campus site. They, therefore, have been unable to subscribe fully to the conclusions reached in paragraph 5.45.

CO-EDUCATION

The present position
5.47 All schools except the two selective schools for the blind provide for both boys and girls.

Evidence received
5.48 The evidence was overwhelmingly in favour of co-education. The headmaster of one school for the blind summed up the general feeling when he said: " It is little use claiming that pupils are being prepared to take their place in the sighted world if they are denied the opportunity of meeting with and talking to young people of the opposite sex during their formative years." An argument advanced in favour particularly of co-education at the primary stage was that, since for many visually handicapped children the recognition of sex differences is very difficult, there is less likelihood of emotional difficulties during adolescence if boys and girls grow up together.

5.49 On the two single-sex schools for the blind, the Governors of Worcester College made points on both sides: " We note the view of the teaching staff that

Mr. G. H. Marshall and Mrs. J. Kell.

there are social, behavioural and academic advantages in a mixed school (and staff room); and that new entrants accustomed to a mixed primary school might well adjust better. On the other hand, we should not ignore the view of the senior boys that co-education would be beneficial only up to the 5th year; and that in the 6th form it could lead to introspection and reluctance to seek the companionship of sighted members of the opposite sex." (While respecting this opinion, we believe that it may be transient). The Governors and staff of Chorleywood however were unequivocal in opposing co-education for their girls. The Governors considered that it would tend " to restrict their social and emotional development to their blind peers, and probably encourage a number of blind girls, who would otherwise marry sighted boys, to marry blind boys." The right course was for the girls to have a single-sex school base from which to go out into the local community, where they can meet sighted members of both sexes and of all ages. The staff considered co-education " particularly hazardous for the blind, who depend so much on ' touch ' and physical contact in their human relationships. There is also the very different rate of development of the two sexes." They would feel happier about co-education at the 6th form level than up to the 5th form.

Consideration of the issues

5.50 We are in no doubt that co-education is desirable for all visually handicapped children throughout, including blind boys and girls pursuing academic courses up to the age of 18 or 19. Since they have been in a mixed primary school, certain—though not all—of the special dangers feared by Chorleywood should be minimised. Some dangers are inevitable; adolescence is a turbulent time even for sighted boys and girls.

ALL-AGE OR SEPARATE PRIMARY AND SECONDARY SCHOOLS

The present position

5.51 Twenty-three out of 39 schools for the visually handicapped are all-age. The proportion for schools for the blind is 3 out of 18, for the partially sighted 18 out of 19, with 2 all-age schools providing for both the blind and the partially sighted. Schools for the blind in the North of England were reorganised in the late 1940s in order to separate provision for primary and for secondary education.

Evidence received

5.52 Witnesses were fairly evenly divided in their opinions. With a very few exceptions, those concerned with providing or running schools favoured the pattern obtaining in their own establishments.

5.53 The chief arguments advanced in favour of the all-age school were that in most areas there were not sufficient children to form viable primary and secondary schools; and that as a result, if these were not all-age schools, some visually handicapped children would have to board away from home. The N.U.T. (no doubt thinking of blind children) said: " Schools for the visually handicapped tend to be regional and, unless they are run on an all-age basis, it is quite possible for a child to have to go up to 100 miles away in order to continue his education when, for example, he moves from infant to primary or primary to secondary work." The ILEA remarked that "even in such a densely populated area, the Authority's schools for the partially sighted are too small to be effectively divided into primary and secondary schools without increasing the length of journeys, which would be detrimental to the children, and the units so created would not be of sufficient size to give enough classes and teachers to provide for pupils with a wide spread of age and ability."

5.54 Other arguments in favour of all-age schools were:

(a) it is harmful for children who have become settled in a school to be uprooted and sent to another one, and some parents dislike it;

(b) continuity of medical and other care. The Society of Medical Officers of Health made this point; and the Governors of the Royal School for the Blind, Liverpool, which is now a primary school, said that visually handicapped children with an additional handicap very often "have complicated hospital programmes to make and to follow;"

(c) flexibility of transfer within the school. The ILEA said: "it is seldom possible to move children up the school strictly by age, and a great deal of flexibility is necessary to deal with the wide variation in degree of handicap and ability which is found in the average partially sighted school;"

(d) the younger children gain confidence from having older children around to lend a helping hand when needed; and

(e) the school is recognised "as a focal point for information and advice for all the visually handicapped in its area."

5.55 The main argument advanced for separate primary and secondary schools was that it is the pattern in ordinary schools; and—in the words of the Headmaster of Henshaw's School for the Blind—"eleven years on the same campus is too long for a blind child in a residential environment and makes too severe a break when the time comes to move on to the next stage of training." Other advantages claimed were that this pattern "allows the primary school academic failure to have a fresh start;" and "the change also widens the experience of the child." The Governors of Worcester College for the Blind consider that "there is a risk inherent in all-age schools that pupils may be retained in the secondary section without impartial assessment for transfer (to a selective school) after the age of eleven."

Consideration of the issues

5.56 We believe that visually handicapped children, particularly the blind, will benefit from a change of environment to widen their experience before going out into the world. In some cases it may be sufficient to secure this at the stage when boys and girls leave school and go on to further education and vocational training. Children who need selective secondary education will necessarily have to move to another school. For many children besides these some of us think that a change of school at 11 or 12 is desirable. Others of us consider that visually handicapped children benefit from the stability of life and the social continuity of an all-age school.

5.57 Since there is some doubt whether all-age schools or separate primary and secondary schools are generally desirable, we suggest that there should be a mixed pattern varying according to local circumstances. All-age schools, however, are in our view certainly preferable where they would enable a substantial proportion of children to attend as day pupils instead of boarding away from home, or as weekly boarders instead of going to a boarding school further away where week-end visits home would be impracticable.

5.58 In what circumstances will the existence of an all-age school make it practicable for children to live at home or, if boarding is inevitable, to be weekly boarders, whereas otherwise they could not? The claim that in most areas there are sufficient visually handicapped children to form viable all-age schools, but not primary and secondary schools, needs to be treated with some caution. Taking partially sighted children in day schools first, if there are fewer than about 80 children of all ages in an area, even an all-age school will not be viable (except where, e.g. on a campus site, teachers for certain subjects can be brought in from other schools); and if there are more than about 100 children, separate primary and secondary schools will be possible. Where however there are about 80-100 partially sighted children in an area, numbers will support an all-age school and only such a school. Schools for the blind are boarding schools and most of them serve a whole region. Where there are about 80–100 blind children in a region, an all-age school might be the only alternative to children going to schools outside the region and thus not being able to go home at week-ends. Moreover, even where numbers would be just enough for separate primary and secondary schools, an all-age school of that number would have a significant advantage in the greater teaching resources that it could call on for the benefit of particular groups of children.

5.59 Where all-age schools are established, there should be flexibility in the age of transfer from the primary department; some children of 11 or 12 have had such a chequered medical history that they are not ready for secondary education. Two points need to be carefully watched—the quality of the secondary education provided and the opportunities for widening children's experience, since it is easy for the atmosphere of a secondary department of an all-age school to become cosy and undemanding. The secondary department needs to be 2-stream if there is to be satisfactory classification of pupils and an adequate range of specialist teaching. The stimulation which can come from a change of school must be secured in other ways. The secondary department of an all-age school should be carefully planned to provide a different environment as well as continuity of care. To enrich the children's experience, teachers should be brought in from other schools on a part-time basis and arrangements should be made for children to participate in lessons and activities of other educational establishments.

SELECTIVE OR COMPREHENSIVE SECONDARY EDUCATION

The present position

5.60 Two single-sex schools for the blind are selective and recruit on a national basis. The Royal Normal College has had a mixed school department taking children of 'average to good intelligence,' but the school is going to close at the

51

end of the summer term, 1972. Exhall Grange serves both as a national grammar school for the partially sighted and as a regional school for partially sighted children who need other types of secondary course.

Evidence received

5.61 The volume of evidence received on this subject was comparatively small. The majority of witnesses were in favour of selection. The chief argument was that, for partially sighted as well as blind children, the number of children suited to academic courses was too small to make it viable to provide, in a number of regional schools, O and A level courses in a variety of subjects. By an ingenious paradox, it was claimed, both for the blind and for the partially sighted, that equality of opportunity with sighted children for the bright child could be ensured only through selection. The RNIB stated that the gifted blind child " needs more specialist teaching, specialist apparatus and specialist amenities if he is to have equal opportunity with the gifted sighted child." The headmaster of one school pointed out that " some partially sighted children of high intelligence may be expected to profit by being at ordinary schools." Another school for the partially sighted, while generally sympathetic to comprehensive schooling, recognised that " whatever reorganisation takes place in day schools to increase secondary opportunities it is likely that not all ' high flyers ' would have full opportunity at local level . . . While the world of employment continues to judge its employees largely on paper qualificatons, the last thing one would want to deny the handicapped is the opportunity to secure the examination results of which they are capable."

5.62 There were however suggestions that Exhall Grange at least should contain a narrower band of ability. One day school proposed that, while the academic courses at Exhall Grange should continue to exist, " the numbers might diminish somewhat and children seeking admission might have more specialised, or perhaps advanced ' A ' level needs." The headmaster of another school did not go as far as this, but he suggested that " non-selective schools should be big enough to provide courses for CSE. Selection for a grammar school is only justified if the pupil selected will be of GCE calibre."

5.63 One of the very few advocates of a comprehensive pattern believed that it was needed for the blind in order to remedy the unfairness of the present system, under which there are wide differences in the standards of the junior departments and schools. On these standards depends success in entry to a selective school, and the range of employment available depends in turn on the type of secondary course taken. The staff of one school for the blind recommended that " the secondary level be wholly comprehensive: 3 or 4 schools serving England and Wales, situated close to the principal centres of population."

Consideration of the issues

5.64 For the reasons given by witnesses, we regard it as inevitable that advanced academic courses should be restricted to a very few schools. There is only a small number of children requiring such courses and there is a shortage of specialist staff. It is important that there should be suitable accommodation for all children likely to profit from GCE ' O ' and ' A ' level work. There has been some difficulty with regard to these courses for partially sighted children considered to be suited to them: some have not been presented for admission to Exhall Grange and others have failed to secure places there. Other schools should be prepared to cater for children who want to take CSE courses. Special arrangements for visually handicapped children taking public examinations are discussed in paragraphs 7.59 to 7.61.

5.65 We consider that the 2 single-sex selective schools for the blind are too small (both have about 70–75 children). There are several ways of meeting this criticism on a co-educational basis. One would be to combine the schools into a single selective school. Another way would be for both to accept a somewhat wider range of ability and vision so as to offer courses for children who develop late and whose interest might be kindled by the presence of brighter children and specialist staff. It would also be possible to turn them into comprehensive schools without interfering with their national intake for academic courses. Just as Exhall Grange serves, for the partially sighted, both as a national grammar school and as a regional school for children requiring other courses, so there could be two other schools with a regional intake for blind children suited to non-academic courses as well as with a national intake for those needing an academic course.

VISUALLY HANDICAPPED CHILDREN WITH ADDITIONAL HANDICAPS

The present position

5.66 All special schools for the visually handicapped contain some children with additional handicaps. The 6 Sunshine Home schools, one primary school (Rushton Hall) and one secondary school (Condover Hall) provide expressly for blind children with additional handicaps; and Condover Hall has a special department (Pathways) admitting about 25 children aged 5–17 with communication problems, who are educationally regarded as having defects of both sight and hearing. The new special schools, which were formed in 1971 out of former training centres and schools in hospitals for the mentally handicapped, contain a number of visually handicapped children. Some indication of the proportion is provided by a survey carried out in the North Midlands in 1970–71 which showed that, out of 2,300 children in the new day special schools (excluding hospital schools), about 80 had a visual handicap. Since 1971 a considerable number of children in other institutions who suffer from both mental and visual handicaps—and possibly others—have been coming to light. In addition, there are units for children with defects of both sight and hearing attached to special or ordinary schools in the London area and Newcastle; and there are 3 special units in hospitals—one admitting 40 mentally handicapped blind children at Reigate in Surrey, one with 30 mentally handicapped blind children, 15 of whom are also deaf (Dr Simon's unit at Lea Hospital, Bromsgrove) and the third with 24 places for maladjusted-blind children of primary age (Dr. Williams' unit at Borocourt Hospital, near Reading). Dr Simon's and Dr Williams' units primarily provide assessment and short-term education.

Evidence received

5.67 The prevalence of additional handicaps is shown in Dr Fine's survey (see paragraph 3.22), which covered children born in or after 1951 attending special schools for the blind or special schools or classes for the partially sighted. Additional handicaps were found in over 50% of the blind children and in over 40% of the partially sighted. Physical handicap was the commonest additional handicap, followed by low intelligence. Although the percentage deemed to be maladjusted was 9% of the blind and 7% of the partially sighted, the teachers interviewed considered 36% of the blind and 32% of the partially sighted to be emotionally disturbed, indicating a need for psychological and psychiatric investigation.

5.68 It was commonly accepted that, where the additional handicaps were mild and the children concerned would fit in with the regime of the general schools for the visually handicapped, these schools could and should accommodate such children. Equally, however, there were some children to whom this did not apply, because their physical or mental handicaps, deafness or maladjustment were so severe. The headmaster of Rushton Hall School, for example, said about children with serious physical handicaps: " A child's natural tendency is to run and dash about and, where sight is sufficient and indeed even with a blind child where other handicaps are not present, this natural tendency is fully exploited. This pace of life can create fear and physical danger in a school society of less ambulant children, and indeed the wheelchair cases can in their turn, provide real hazards to the fully mobile ones." Again, a severely disturbed child could disrupt the life of an entire school. The headmaster of Tapton Mount said that " some of these disturbed children are of a high order of intelligence and in desperate need of help."

5.69 The solutions suggested for these visually and multiply handicapped children who are not suited to the general schools for the visually handicapped were broadly four:

(i) separate schools or small units for children suffering from a particular combination of handicaps, in the way that Pathways caters for children who are educationally regarded as having defects of both sight and hearing; (Dr Simon, for example, suggested that there should be 4 assessment centres in or attached to hospitals, to each of which would be linked 4 small units, attached to special schools, for children suffering from mental handicap, deafness and blindness).

(ii) for partially sighted children, separate departments or classes in the general schools for the partially sighted;

(iii) for partially sighted children, where the visual handicap is the minor one, accommodation in special schools dealing with their major handicaps;

(iv) schools for the visually and multiply handicapped. The headmaster of Rushton Hall said: " In a school specially designed for multiple handicaps, a whole range of specialist services can be, and is, laid on."

5.70 In most countries overseas no special provision is made for multiply-handicapped blind children. In the U.S.A. schools for the blind contain a large proportion of multiply-handicapped children. One enquiry by Bucknam[10] showed that in one residential school 70% of the children had additional handicaps, and 33% had IQs below 80.

Consideration of the issues

5.71 In view of the many different combinations of handicaps possible, with different degrees of severity, we believe that a variety of provision is essential for visually handicapped children with additional handicaps. Where the additional handicaps are predominant and prevent a child from fitting into the normal pattern of a school for visually handicapped children, day special schools for the multiply handicapped should be prepared to admit some of these children provided that their visual handicap is recognised and specialised care is maintained. We recognise however that there will be some children whose combination of handicaps would not enable them to fit into either a general school for visually handicapped children or a special school for the multiply handicapped. There will consequently be a continuing need for a few schools specifically for visually handicapped children with additional handicaps. For particular combinations of handicaps, either a single unit like Pathways serving the whole country or a number of strategically situated ones is required. We believe that some of the mentally handicapped blind children need to be accommodated in special local units; and that several more units are required outside the Midlands to accommodate children suffering from mental handicap, deafness and blindness, on the lines of Dr Simon's unit. Since Dr Williams' unit for the maladjusted-blind is usually not full, the only further provision needed for these children is somewhere where they can receive education and treatment for as long as they require it.

CONCLUSIONS

5.72 Several general ideas emerge from our thinking about the different aspects of the organisation of schools. One is that visually handicapped children ought, wherever practicable, to live at home and attend schools by day; where this is impracticable, weekly boarding is the best system. A second general idea is that the provision of education and child care could be improved by accommodating various groups of children together (or perhaps in different units on the same site) rather than separately. We support co-education, the education of blind and partially sighted children in the same schools, and all-age schools in certain circumstances. While we believe that only a very few schools can cater satisfactorily for children requiring an advanced academic course, we can see advantages in these children forming part of larger units than the existing two single-sex grammar schools for the blind, possibly with a wider range of ability. Again, it seems unavoidable that some visually handicapped children with very severe additional handicaps should attend specialised schools, but we think that some children with serious additional handicaps could fit well into day schools catering for multiply handicapped children. Another general idea is that ordinary schools should play a bigger part in the education of visually handicapped children. Thus, we favour further systematic experiments in educating some of these children in

---

[10] Bucknam, F. G. Multiple-handicapped blind children (an incidence survey). The International Journal for the Education of the Blind, 15 December, 1965, pp. 46–49.

ordinary schools; and special schools preparing children to take public examinations should be able to draw on the specialist facilities of neighbouring secondary schools for sighted children.

5.73 The existing pattern of schools for the visually handicapped will require to be altered in many respects if our recommendations are to be put into practice. In the next chapter we shall consider the need for a further fundamental change—in the management of schools—and for a national plan to be drawn up for the development of schools on the lines we favour.

RECOMMENDATIONS

5.74 We recommend that:

(1) all blind and partially sighted children, except some of those with multiple handicaps or poor home conditions, should live at home if their home is within an hour's journey of a suitable school and provided their parents can be given guidance on child management (paragraph 5.09);

(2) where day attendance is impracticable, weekly boarding should be adopted and local education authorities should help with travel home (paragraph 5.10);

(3) all boarding schools should be prepared to accept children, who normally attend school by day, for boarding for short periods to meet domestic emergencies (paragraph 5.12);

(4) further systematic experiments should be carried out, within the context of the national plan (see Chapter 6), with the education of visually handicapped children in ordinary schools, either in ordinary or in special classes (paragraph 5.31);

(5) experiments are desirable, in order to meet regional needs, in the grouping of several schools for children with different handicaps on campus sites, sharing a full range of educational and medical resources, with ordinary schools adjoining (paragraphs 5.36–5.37);

(6) [11]blind and partially sighted children would benefit from being educated in the same schools, though they need to be in separate classes at the junior stage (paragraph 5.45);

(7) co-education should be adopted for all visually handicapped children throughout their school careers (paragraph 5.50);

(8) all-age schools are to be preferred where their existence would enable a substantial proportion of children to attend as day pupils instead of boarding away from home, or as weekly boarders instead of going to a boarding school further away where week-end visits home would be impracticable. Otherwise, there should be a mixed pattern of all-age schools and separate primary and secondary schools, varying according to local circumstances (paragraph 5.57);

---

[11] Two members dissent from this recommendation.

(9) places should be provided for all visually handicapped children likely to profit from GCE ' O ' and ' A ' level work; courses would be required in only a very few schools, none of which should be as small as the 2 single-sex selective schools for the blind. Other schools should be prepared to cater for children who want to take CSE courses etc. (paragraphs 5.64–5.65); and

(10) a variety of special schools and units should be available for visually handicapped children with additional handicaps. Where such children are accommodated in special schools for the multiply handicapped, due attention and care must be given to their visual handicap (paragraph 5.71).

E

CHAPTER 6 : A NATIONAL PLAN FOR SPECIAL SCHOOLS AND OTHER EDUCATIONAL SERVICES FOR THE VISUALLY HANDICAPPED

6.01 In this chapter we turn to the management and distribution of schools and the arrangements for co-ordinating the national provision.

The present position

6.02 The education of the blind is the only field of special education in which more than half the provision is made by voluntary bodies. Out of 20 schools (2 of which have a department for the partially sighted and so are counted again in the number of schools for the partially sighted), 17 are managed by voluntary bodies. The Royal National Institute for the Blind is responsible for 10 schools (including 6 Sunshine Home schools), but no other body manages more than one school. There are also 3 establishments for the further education and training of the blind, all run by voluntary bodies. Out of 21 schools for the partially sighted, 4 are managed by voluntary bodies.

6.03 The distribution of schools for the blind is very uneven. An undue proportion is in the North West, Midlands and South East. Many of the schools are situated in rural areas.

Evidence received

6.04 Although we did not specifically seek evidence on the management, general organisation and distribution of schools for the visually handicapped, 3 bodies and 4 individuals submitted their views. Several of these suggested that deficiencies in the educational services for the visually handicapped were attributable to the present system whereby only one voluntary body has experience of managing more than one school. Some witnesses stated that the schools administered by the voluntary bodies were on the whole poorly managed, and tended to have closer relations with their parent bodies than with neighbouring ordinary schools and the sighted community at large. There was also some criticism of the geographical remoteness of some schools for the blind and of their distribution.

6.05 The suggestion most frequently put to us in evidence as to future organisation was that all non-maintained schools, while remaining outside the maintained system, should be covered by some kind of nationally co-ordinated plan for schools for the visually handicapped. How this might operate in practice was not always made clear, but the RNIB suggested " the establishment of some kind of central advisory body which can oversee needs and implement the most effective use of all the services having regard to changing circumstances and social educational attitudes," though acknowledging that " this body would not be wholly effective without powers of co-ordination and direction." There were also a few more radical proposals that the non-maintained schools be taken over altogether, either by local education authorities, by regional bodies or by a central body.

Consideration of the issues

6.06 The position of the non-maintained schools is unsatisfactory in a number of ways. We appreciate the important pioneer role played by voluntary bodies in developing education for the visually handicapped, and the devotion and skill shown by those responsible for administering non-maintained schools. It is important that the experience acquired should continue to be used and that the active goodwill and practical support of the voluntary organisations should be preserved. Nevertheless, we agree with the views expressed in the evidence received that some schools suffer from an isolation that is educational and social as well as geographical. They lack adequate contacts with other schools and educational institutions; and the teachers tend to be outside the mainstream of their profession. Nor do schools have behind them the resources of a local education authority in advisory staff, educational equipment, building expertise etc. It is probably not conducive to efficiency that, apart from the RNIB, no voluntary body runs more than one school; and some governing bodies contain few members with much claim to educational knowledge.

6.07 We believe that a number of the voluntary bodies would not be averse to securing relief from the financial burden of administering their schools. If schools were taken over by local education authorities, early guidance would be required from the Department of Education and Science on the financial terms appropriate. The arrangements for transfer would vary from school to school in the light of the particular circumstances of each, including the terms of any charitable trust under which a school was provided and the extent to which the governing body was concerned with other aspects of the welfare of the visually handicapped. The following ways were suggested in which the voluntary bodies' great experience in this field could still be used and their support maintained for the education of both the blind and the partially sighted:

(a) active participation in the management of schools, through membership of their governing bodies or through personal involvement in services such as reading and transcribing;

(b) the production of braille books, tapes, cassettes etc. and the evaluation and provision of apparatus and equipment on a national scale; and

(c) the provision of services. Some services are best supplied locally, but others need country-wide knowledge, or resources or expertise that could not be found in many places. Examples are: professional careers advice; services for university and college students; bursaries and scholarships for travel and advanced studies; and research.

6.08 At the same time, it is to be expected that some voluntary bodies would wish to continue to manage their schools. A school is often a source of pride to the body which has set it up, and it acts as a magnet when an appeal for public support is made for the general activities of the voluntary body. It would be regrettable if, as a result of giving up their schools, some voluntary bodies found that they were so impoverished that they were unable to provide the supporting services mentioned in paragraph 6.07.

6.09 Under existing legislation, the implementation of a policy to transfer any of the schools would depend on persuading the voluntary bodies and the LEAs to play their part. The Secretary of State has certain powers under the Education Acts: he is responsible for approving special schools, and he can make it a condition of his approval not merely that a school should provide places that are needed for handicapped pupils but that it should be situated in a suitable location for meeting this need. Further, the Handicapped Pupils and Special Schools Regulations, 1959, require that a non-maintained special school should be " under the direction of a body of managers composed of a sufficient number of suitably qualified persons " (Reg. 19(1)). It is the responsiblity of LEAs to secure that provision is made for special educational treatment for pupils in their areas who suffer from any disability of mind or body. At present, however, the Department of Education and Science would be most unlikely to withdraw recognition from any non-maintained special school under its present management, so long as its educational standards were high and the places it provided were required. Equally, the Department cannot force a local education authority to open a new special school or to take over an existing non-maintained one.

6.10 The difficult problems to be resolved of the management and distribution of schools, with the far-reaching alterations in the internal organisation of schools that we advocate in Chapter 5, have convinced us that some special machinery is needed to implement our ideas and to bring about the changes required in the school pattern. We propose that a national plan should be drawn up for special schools and other educational services for the visually handicapped. Wide participation in the work seems to us important: not only would it ensure that full account was taken of local needs and circumstances but also it should help to foster a commitment to carry out the plan. The Department of Education and Science should begin by designating regions of the country in each of which a regional committee would be set up representing LEAs within the region. After consultation with representatives of voluntary bodies and of the health services, each regional committee should prepare plans on both a short-term and a long-term basis for the reorganisation of schools and other educational services for visually handicapped children in its regions. At least in some cases, the existing regional conferences on handicapped children might serve as regional committees for this purpose. The Department would have the functions of co-ordinating the different regional plans; consulting DHSS as necessary on any medical questions; determining which schools should draw children from all over the country; and establishing a national committee to promote and oversee the execution of the national plan.

6.11 We will now explain in more detail certain aspects of our proposals. By plans on a short-term basis, we mean plans for the better and more economical use of existing buildings and services without moving schools to new sites. We believe that there is considerable scope for such rationalisation. It may help if we give two hypothetical examples. Where a selective school is too small, one of the suggestions made in paragraph 5.65 was that it should accept a somewhat wider range of ability and vision. Again it might help a school for the partially sighted to accommodate some partially sighted children from its area who at present cannot obtain admission if it could transfer some children near the borderline between partial sight and blindness to a school for the blind in the same region with empty places.

6.12 By plans on a long-term basis, we mean plans for the optimum organisation, distribution and management of schools and services, including the 3 establishments for the further education and training of the blind. If schools are redistributed on a regional basis (apart from those performing a national function), it will prevent many children from having to attend schools at long distances from their homes. Many of the buildings of the Sunshine Home Schools for the blind are no longer suitable for their purpose. There is scope for replacing these by a number of probably smaller residential units carefully sited in regard to population and communications, which would offer a completely flexible service to the young blind child.

6.13 The regional committees might wish to consider whether the needs of their region would be served by a closer grouping of schools for the visually handicapped, perhaps to the extent of concentrating most of the schools in the region on one or more campus sites near centres of population with good communications, with certain other types of educational provision close at hand. The advantages and disadvantages of such a pattern of provision were discussed in paragraph 5.36. We agreed that experiments on these lines would be valuable.

6.14 We believe that the impetus, the resources and the goodwill required to bring about radical changes over a period of years can be generated if the national plan meets with a general welcome and if it is accepted that it provides a sensible framework for all future developments. At the same time, the improvements which the national plan may be expected to bring about in the education of the visually handicapped are too important for their implementation to be left in the last resort to the wishes of individual bodies. As we have already pointed out, negotiation over the transfer of an individual school between the Department on the one hand and a voluntary body and a local education authority (or authorities) on the other is doomed to failure if either of the latter cannot be persuaded to accept the proposal for that school in the national plan. We consider therefore that the Secretary of State should be empowered, if necessary by new legislation, to ensure that the recommendations of the national plan are put into effect within a reasonable period of time.

6.15 So far we are all agreed. A divergence of view has, however, been revealed about the vexed question whether or not ALL non-maintained special schools for the visually handicapped should be transferred to local education authorities. The majority of us consider that the future of these schools could best be determined pragmatically and piecemeal within the context of the national plan. Any school could remain under its present management if (a) it were recognised to be efficiently conducted and (b) either it fitted into the long-term plan for its region or the voluntary body maintaining it were willing to move it to the new site proposed in the plan. If these conditions were not fulfilled, the regional committee (supported, where necessary, by the national committee) should ascertain the willingness of the responsible body to give up its school and should seek an authority ready to take the school over. If the voluntary body were unwilling, or if it were willing but no authority could be found to take on the school, the regional committee would still include its proposal, with a statement to that effect, in its regional contribution to the national plan. Compulsion would then be used in the last resort, as explained in paragraph 6.14, to secure the implementation of this part of the plan.

6.16 Five members[1] consider that the education of the visually handicapped ought to be more demonstrably a national responsibility. They believe that not only are many schools run by voluntary bodies isolated and backed by inadequate educational and medical resources, but also that some parents would prefer not to have what they regard as a " charity " education for their children. In the view of these members, the only way to make these schools effectively a national responsibility and to bring them into the mainstream of education is to transfer them all to local education authorities, whether or not they could be fitted into the national plan under their present management. To this end, the transfer of all the schools should be laid down as an integral feature of the national plan.

Recommendations

6.17 We recommend that:

(1) a national plan should be drawn up for the distribution, organisation and management of special schools and other educational services for the visually handicapped (paragraph 6.10);

(2) to this end, committees representing the local education authorities should be set up, in regions designated by the Department of Education and Science, to prepare plans on both a short-term and a long-term basis for their region, after consultation with representatives of voluntary bodies and the health services (paragraph 6.10);

(3) the Department should co-ordinate the regional plans, determine which schools should have a countrywide intake, and establish a national committee to promote and oversee the execution of the national plan (paragraph 6.10); and

(4) the Secretary of State should be empowered, if necessary by new legislation, to ensure that the recommendations of the national plan are put into effect within a reasonable period of time (paragraph 6.14).

---

[1] Dr D. Cook, Mr G. Exley, Mr R. Gulliford, Mr C. R. Harris and Mr G. H. Marshall. Three members expressed no opinion on the subject.

CHAPTER 7: CURRICULUM AND TEACHING AIDS

INTRODUCTION

7.01 Our general invitation to submit evidence sought views on many curricular questions, and in addition we set up two working parties, one on the curriculum for the blind and the other on the curriculum for the partially sighted, which sent detailed questionnaires to all schools. Despite the volume of evidence, we have been impressed by the relatively few points on which there has been any fundamental disagreement. We have also noted with approval how many developments in the curriculum for the visually handicapped are already taking place, many of them as a result of ingenious approaches devised by the schools and teachers themselves from their own experience. We have not thought it right to consider in any very great detail the finer points of curriculum content: in many cases the curriculum must be very closely geared to the particular needs of individual children, and there are therefore large areas in which teachers must exercise their discretion in determining what they teach and how they teach it. Furthermore, in some instances the most suitable teaching approach and curriculum content can be satisfactorily determined only after conducting research which it has properly been no part of our task to carry out. We have thus concentrated on offering more general guidance and indicating some of the areas where research is most urgently needed. It has not been possible to discuss specifically the problems presented by the education of multiply handicapped children, since these vary so widely according to the additional handicap.

7.02 We have taken a fairly broad approach to the curriculum, and have not restricted ourselves to what might be termed the more academic side of a child's life at school. We consider first the more important general aspects of the curriculum and the use of teaching aids, and then examine some of the problems posed by individual subjects. In this chapter we have not followed our usual pattern of setting out under separate headings the present position, evidence received and our consideration of the issues. The reason is that so many detailed topics need to be touched on briefly under each broad heading (like reading and writing, the range of books available and aids to teaching and learning) that it would interfere with the flow of the argument and fragment the chapter if the usual tripartite division were used. We have however tried to follow the usual order as far as possible within individual paragraphs.

CLASS GROUPING IN SCHOOLS FOR THE VISUALLY HANDICAPPED

7.03 In January, 1971, out of 111 classes for the blind 23 had an age span of 3 years or more and out of 142 for the partially sighted 73 had age spans of 3 years or more. In the schools for the blind and partially sighted together there were 20 classes, 11 with an age span of 3 years or more. It is noticeable that the larger schools tend to avoid wide age spans in their classes. In class groupings the choice is of course between grouping by age and by ability, and in determining its own pattern each school must have regard to the efficient deployment of its teaching resources. Many of the schools for the visually handicapped are small, and most of them have a very wide ability range. However, a very wide ability range within a single class can occasion very real difficulties for the teacher. We consider that schools should be flexible in their groupings but they should generally adopt a system of ability-setting in academic subjects.

READING AND WRITING FOR THE BLIND

7.04 The main medium of reading and writing for blind children is braille, which is a system based on six raised dots, various combinations of which denote letters, words, contractions (signs standing for two or more letters in a word) and punctuation. The 63 possible permutations are assigned a total of 201 ' meanings ', some combinations having to serve more than one purpose—thus, a sign may denote a letter, word, or contraction according to its position in the word. There are two grades: Grade II includes all the signs and contractions possible; Grade I uses 42 of them, each standing for either an alphabetical letter or a punctuation sign and carrying but one interpretation, and no contractions are employed. We asked one of our members to conduct on our behalf a survey of braille reading in schools for the blind (see Appendix F). The survey covered 625 pupils aged 10 to 18. It was found that approximately 40% of those from 10 to 16 years were unable to complete satisfactorily the silent reading test administered. The number of pupils in the sample with low general ability contributed substantially to this high rate of failure. When reading ability was measurable, the rate of reading was found to progress steadily with age, from a mean of 78 words per minute at age 11 to 103 words at 16.

7.05 These reading speeds were very much slower on average than those of a small control group of sighted children. The comprehension of the blind readers, however, was not significantly different from that of sighted children. We also sent out to schools a questionnaire on the teaching of braille, which revealed fairly wide variations in practice. Few schools used Grade I, most of them preferring to use Grade II from the outset, but there was no standard order for the introduction of letters and contractions. Among the general evidence which we received on braille the consensus of opinion was that it should be introduced to children at as early a stage as they could manage and that there was no " best method " of teaching it. A common complaint in evidence was the unsuitability of early reading schemes in braille.

7.06 All blind children should be given a fair trial with braille. There is no reason why those of average general ability who possess adequate tactile discrimination should not reach a standard of reading comprehension equal to that of their sighted contemporaries, though it would seem inevitable that in using braille their rate of reading will be slower. In addition to the extra time required to read each word and sentence, the blind child is impeded by an inability to scan the page quickly, which makes selective reading almost impossible. (The implications of this for examinations for visually handicapped children are considered in paragraph 7.61). Because of such disadvantage, inherent in a tactile medium of reading, it is imperative that there should be made available

64

supplementary media for obtaining information, for example, talking books (see paragraph 7.23) or a device like the Optacon[1]. The increase in the number of blind children with additional handicaps, which in some instances can debar the attainment of any fluency in braille reading, highlights the need for other media.

7.07 Some of the evidence we received suggested that braille reading and writing are often not begun in the first year or two at school. This is understandable since many young children when they first enter school are not ready to learn to read, particularly through the medium of braille. Various activities leading to reading are undertaken, alongside games involving sorting and matching to help to develop tactile discrimination. Further investigation is required into the optimum developmental age level for the beginning of formal teaching in braille reading and writing[2] (see Chapter 10).

7.08 There has been considerable disagreement about the value of employing Grade II from the beginning. Research studies by Nolan and Kederis[3] have indicated that in braille reading separate characters must be subsequently integrated, and that these should be taught first by Grade I before proceeding to Grade II. Other studies[4] also suggest that there may be advantage in reducing the number of contractions in Grade II, since many of these occur infrequently in children's books. A programme of research is urgently needed into all aspects of braille teaching, particularly into the relative merits of Grade I and Grade II for beginners (see Chapter 10).

7.09 For braille writing, the Perkins brailler has been found to be of great value and these machines are now in widespread use in all schools for the blind. Every child should possess one of these machines and should retain it when he leaves school. The brailler is, however, not equally useful in all circumstances: for note taking, for example, a blind person may have to use lighter and quieter apparatus, a braille pocket frame or Banks writer or an easily portable cassette tape recorder. The use of the pocket frame is a special skill, since it requires each character to be written backwards and with a special implement. We consider that all schools should instruct in the use of the pocket frame at an appropriate age all children who are able to make progress with it and who are likely to find it of value either at school or thereafter. At a later stage portable cassette tape recorders should be available to all children.

7.10 It is obviously desirable that blind people should be able to communicate in writing with the sighted, but braille is not generally useful for this purpose.

---

[1] A device called the Optacon has been developed at the Stanford Research Institute, U.S.A. In this, print or any other visual material is scanned by a minute television camera, and then translated into patterns of vibrations which the reader feels with his hand. The pattern reproduces exactly the shapes of the letters, etc. in the visual material. This device is being used successfully by a few selected blind children and adults, but much further investigation is required to discover how widely it could be used with good effect. Thus it is at present not generally available, but controlled experiments are now under way in this country.

[2] A recent experiment has shown that, in the conditions of the experiment, blind people read braille significantly faster with the left hand than with the right (Hermelin, B. and O'Connor, N. — 1971, Nature, Vol. 231, 470).

[3] Nolan, C. Y. and Kederis, C. J. (1969). Perceptual factors in braille word recognition. Research Series No. 20, American Foundation for the Blind.

[4] Cited by Lorimer, J., Teacher of the Blind 1972, Vol. 60, No. 2.

To do this the only alternatives are handwriting and typewriting. The evidence we received showed that handwriting is very little used in schools for the blind beyond teaching children how to sign their names, and more might be done. Many children may have sufficient vision to write and they should be encouraged to write if at all possible. But undoubtedly the best hope is typewriting, which incidentally helps to eradicate spelling difficulties caused by learning through braille alone with its contractions. Most schools for the blind do in fact teach typing, and we consider that it should be taught to all children who can become proficient at it. It could be introduced during the primary stage, depending on the child's ability, and all children who have learnt to type should be able to take their own typewriter with them on leaving school.

READING AND WRITING FOR THE PARTIALLY SIGHTED

7.11 To the layman written communication with the partially sighted may seem to present fewer problems than with the blind since the partially sighted use the same medium as sighted children. However, learning to read and write is an altogether more painstaking process for the partially sighted than for the sighted child, and there are several important points which should not be overlooked. The evidence which we received on reading and writing for the partially sighted revealed few controversial issues. The most frequent general observation was that reading standards among partially sighted children were significantly lower than standards among sighted children. Like blind children, partially sighted children are likely to fall well below the reading speeds of sighted children, but the partially sighted child may also be slow to master the basic techniques of reading. He may suffer from restriction of peripheral vision which makes scanning difficult and which would prevent him from seeing even quite short words in context, and from seeing longer words as a whole. Such problems may both limit the acquisition of reading speed and hinder the attainment of normal reading standards. Thus particular attention should be given in schools with partially sighted children to the teaching of reading with special regard to the defects of individual children; and staffing should be sufficiently generous to allow periods of individual tuition geared to any special difficulties. Information will need to be given to teachers on the educational implications of each individual child's defect.

7.12 Some partially sighted children can be helped in learning to read by the use of low visual aids to magnify print. There is some evidence that schools, though equipped with these aids, do not in fact use them very much. We consider that no partially sighted child should lack any low visual aid which may help him, and that all schools should be fully equipped with appropriate low visual aids which are kept in good order (Appendix E gives information about these aids). Advice on individual cases should be obtained from the school ophthalmologist. It is also important that the books used should be clearly printed on a good, white matt surface.

7.13 Some schools for the partially sighted at present teach braille, but only to those few children at risk of becoming blind or almost blind. In evidence submitted to us there was much disagreement over whether braille should be taught more widely to partially sighted children. On the one hand, it was said that partially sighted children should be encouraged to make the maximum possible use of whatever vision they have and should not therefore learn braille unless there is a chance that they may lose that vision. On the other hand, it was argued that many partially sighted children find reading by visual methods so difficult that they are never likely to turn to printed material in later life for recreation, and should therefore have braille available to them as an alternative. We take the view that, for leisure reading, recorded books have such advantages over braille material (see paragraph 7.23) that adding instruction in braille to an already very full curriculum for partially sighted children cannot be justified by recreational needs alone. We therefore agree that braille should not be taught to partially sighted children apart from those whose vision is—or may become— so bad that they cannot read print. For teaching braille to such children, schools for the partially sighted should be able to call on the services of qualified teachers of the blind.

7.14 In learning to write it is especially difficult for the partially sighted child to imitate the flow of his teacher's handwriting. Overhead projectors have proved invaluable in throwing up large images which the partially sighted child can follow easily, and all schools should make use of them under proper conditions. Particular attention should also be paid to the quality and colour of writing paper and the type of pen used by the child. Some partially sighted children will find typing very much easier than handwriting and the results are much more legible, but handwriting should not be neglected. Like blind children, partially sighted children should be introduced to typewriting as soon as practicable. All children who have learnt to type should be allowed to have their own machine on leaving school.

THE RANGE OF BOOKS AVAILABLE TO VISUALLY HANDICAPPED CHILDREN

7.15 The evidence we received was unanimous in criticising provision of books for blind and partially sighted children. This was indeed the most frequently made complaint in the evidence which we received on the curriculum and it occurred again and again in comments on difficulties relating to particular subjects. It therefore seems appropriate to comment on this as a general aspect of the curriculum separately from our consideration of the acquisition and practice of reading and writing skills, though it is obviously closely related to these.

7.16 Books for the partially sighted need to be carefully selected and they are often expensive; there is therefore a need for a high per capita allowance to be made to the schools. The partially sighted have nobody like the RNIB to assist in the production of suitable books, and they have to rely on what may be available from libraries and what they can produce themselves. Most public libraries make a number of clearly printed books available. These, however, can only meet part of the need, since it is quite rightly no part of the function of public libraries to supply text books for use in schools. Schools may need to enlarge certain types of material, e.g. small print books and mathematical symbols. Schools therefore need access to an enlarger and—because of the importance of good type-definition in multiple reproduction—to offset litho copying equipment. Again, the main problem is one of cost: although ideally each school for the partially sighted should have its own equipment, we recognise that limited resources may make this impossible. There are, however, ways of overcoming this difficulty. The Inner London and Birmingham Education Authorities, for example, both concentrate enlarging and copying equipment at one of their schools for the partially sighted. Elsewhere, authorities should consider whether they might group together on a regional basis to make production of clearly printed material a joint task. If this is not practicable, production could be made more economic by making a partially sighted school's equipment available on a shared-time basis to local educational establishments for the sighted. Alternatively, the printing department of the local authority might help if it has facilities for enlargement and clear print.

7.17 Braille books are both bulky and expensive. This was forcefully illustrated in one piece of evidence to us which pointed out that a small dictionary, measuring 5" x 3½" x 1" and costing only 30p in print, transcribed into 16 braille volumes, measuring 10" x 13" x 28", weighing 45 lbs. and costing in all £16. These prices and size differentials themselves impose very severe limitations on both the production and use of braille books. The facilities of the RNIB for the supply of books are fully stretched and cannot always respond very quickly to demand. At present the RNIB is producing each year 100 to 150 titles in multiple copies and adding just over 1,000 new titles to the Students' Braille Library. This compares with new editions and titles of printed books in this country of some 30,000 each year. The deficiency in the supply of braille books has obvious consequences for the schools. Books are either unobtainable or obtainable only many months after they are required; the extreme cost leads to a reluctance to discard books, even when they may have become out of date, producing storage problems; and, most important, there is an inevitable tendency to let the present availability of books determine the content of the teaching.

7.18 Among the books most commonly said to be in short supply in braille are sets of text books, especially at advanced level, reference books, foreign language books, and general reading books. Many schools remedy some of the worst deficiencies by producing their own braille material, using a thermoform duplicator. There is also a need for some form of braille reproduction—not necessarily thermoplastic, which has some limitations—and a technician to operate the equipment. We have been much impressed by a report of a Dutch school with an extensive system of voluntary help in book production. This kind of arrangement is sometimes encountered in British schools. Certain schools receive help from the inmates of local prisons and from friends of the school. Other schools might consider whether they could enlist similar help. Schools should also make greater efforts to help one another by circulating among themselves details of the braille material which they have been able to obtain or to produce themselves. Although book supply could be considerably improved by the arrangements we have just described, they are still unsatisfactory stop-gap measures. Formal arrangements for the production and supply of braille books need to be greatly extended. There is a number of ways in which this might be achieved. In Sweden the Government set up in 1969 a company called Swedish Educational Products Limited, in which it has a 50% share and which produces, among other things, braille books.

7.19 We recommend that the appropriate Government departments should take urgent steps to ensure that the production of books for both the blind and the partially sighted is fully adequate. Investigation and development of new printing methods of braille are also required (see Chapter 10).

AIDS TO TEACHING AND LEARNING

7.20 We have received much evidence relating to the provision of aids to teaching and learning in schools for the visually handicapped. They have revealed much ingenuity and effort on the part of the individual schools and teachers to meet particular needs which have arisen, but the overall picture has been one of shortage. One of the undoubted difficulties is that many of the aids are expensive. The value of some aids to teaching and learning is restricted to one or two particular subjects, and we return to these below. However, many of them are of more general application, as for example audio teaching aids for the blind, low visual aids for individual children to make the best use of their residual vision, audio-visual teaching aids for children with some sight and programmed learning devices.

7.21 Schools for the visually handicapped rely very largely on audio aids, but it must not be forgotten that full use needs to be made of a child's residual vision. The audio aids available are programmes transmitted for schools on radio (and sometimes on television), gramophone records and tape recorders. The schools programmes are, of course, usually devised with sighted children in mind, and often need adaptation for use with blind children. At present, the staff of schools for the blind make highly commendable efforts to tape and edit programmes to make them more suitable. There seems little alternative to the schools' making some such arrangements of their own, though much time of the teaching staff could be saved if more technicians were available. Schools could also use tape recorders to record broadcast programmes or series of programmes which they find valuable. All visually handicapped children should be instructed in the use of a tape recorder and there would be great merit in arrangements for each child who can use one to have his own cassette tape recorder on leaving school. Early training in the use of pocket tape recorders for note-taking would be of value to many pupils; these are extensively used by pupils at Tapton Mount School taking part in the integrated education experiment (see paragraph 5.22).

7.22 Blind students in higher education receive supporting services from the RNIB including the use of the Students' Braille and Tape Libraries. Even so, it is probable that these will be unable to provide all the material required. Students will need the services of sighted readers either to read to them directly or to dictate the material on open tape. It is helpful if lecturers allow them to record notes on a small battery tape recorder or to use a braille shorthand or Banks-writer, but no braille machine is completely silent. Students studying technical or statistical subjects need to produce and interpret diagrams, maps and graphs and require equipment to reproduce these fairly quickly in embossed form. If there is much statistical calculation to be done, an Odhner Calculator, adapted with braille markings, should be available. A typewriter with mathematical symbols is useful for students studying mathematics.

7.23 Talking books for the visually handicapped are in essence books recorded on tape, but normally only authorised visually handicapped readers using special machines are permitted to have them. There is now a good deal of evidence, principally from the United States, that talking books are a very valuable tool for use with the blind, not only for recreation, but for learning purposes also. June Morris[5] in the USA and M. J. Tobin[6] in this country showed that the learning efficiency of blind children (that is the amount learned per unit of time spent) in social studies, literature and science was very much greater with talking books than with braille material. There is no doubt that children must continue to learn braille as a first priority. Talking books can never satisfactorily replace braille versions of some books, including those to which children need to make regular reference, such as dictionaries and standard text-books. Braille will also be needed for writing, since dictating on to tapes will not always be a suitable alternative. Nevertheless, there would appear prima facie to be a very strong case for greater use of talking books in schools for the blind. We would urge that titles specially suited to children should be added to the talking book service as soon as possible and its facilities made available to all children. Talking books may also be of value with the partially sighted, particularly for leisure reading outside school or after leaving school. At present, however, there are no arrangements for the supply of talking books to the partially sighted, and we urge that the same facilities should be provided for them. Consideration of the best means of producing talking books and other recorded books should take into account the arrangements for the supply of braille books (see paragraph 7.18); it may well be that the same arrangements for finance and production can apply to both. At the same time, further research should be initiated into the relative effectiveness of the braille and talking book media for teaching different subjects to children of varying age and intelligence (see Chapter 10).

7.24 It has been shown that the efficiency of learning may in certain circumstances be improved by the use of tape recorded material and children need to be taught how to make the maximum use of this. An important part of a visually handicapped child's education is the art of listening which he should acquire from an early age. Language laboratories can be used for purposes other than the acquisition of foreign languages (see paragraph 7.36).

7.25 We have already referred to low visual aids (including spectacles) for partially sighted children in connection with learning to read (paragraph 7.12). Dr Fine's survey of partially sighted children showed that some 59% used spectacles only, and that relatively little use was made of other low visual aids. Different kinds of low visual aid are required for the various types of defect in the partially sighted; and there are some children for whom low visual aids are not appropriate, either because of the nature or degree of their handicap. However, many children could benefit greatly and we find it depressing that schools do not make the fullest use of them (for further discussion see Appendix E).

---

[5] Morris, June E. Relative efficiency of reading and listening for braille and large type readers. Conference of the American Association of Instructors of the Blind, 1966. (This study also showed that partially sighted children learnt better with talking books than with printed material).

[6] Tobin, M. J. et al. Programmed learning for the child. Education of the Visually Handicapped, 1970, 2, 11.

7.26 Lighting is of the utmost importance to children who use sighted methods of learning. It is not appropriate for us to consider the technical details of lighting in this report, but the prime consideration for schools must be to ensure that there is good general lighting and a fully adjustable system of individual lighting either at the desk or overhead. The schools should bear in mind that the effectiveness of good lighting can be nullified by deterioration in lighting power and by dull or dirty reflecting surfaces; on the other hand surfaces must not be so highly reflecting as to produce glare. There is already much experience of lighting both in the United Kingdom and overseas; and advice on the most appropriate lighting arrangements is available from the Department of Education and Science. DES Building Bulletin No. 33, " Lighting in Schools " (available from HMSO) also includes an appendix on schools for partially sighted children.

7.27 Some visually handicapped children are also very sensitive to noise and good hearing conditions are essential particularly for multi-handicapped children. There is therefore a need to provide non-resonant surfaces in the classroom.

7.28 Audio-visual aids can be of great help in teaching the partially sighted. At Exhall Grange School the audio-visual centre had a very wide range of equipment, all of which is found of great value. This includes overhead projectors, back projection facilities to enable children to stand or sit very close to a screen, slide projectors and tape-linked slide projectors, film projectors and video tape recorders. Because much of this equipment is so costly, Exhall Grange is fortunate in its facilities; but what has been done at this school shows what is possible elsewhere provided adequate finance is forthcoming. In small schools the per capita cost of installing all this equipment would be very high, but costs could be reduced by amalgamation of schools or the grouping of schools with a shared audio-visual centre. Again, schools for the partially sighted could well share resources with neighbouring sighted schools or with colleges of further education. The aim should be for even the smallest schools to have a reasonable supply of audio-visual aids, and local authorities and other maintaining bodies should accept the need for fairly considerable capital expenditure and maintenance costs. Appendix G gives more information about audio-visual aids.

7.29 It has been suggested to us that programmed learning can be of great value with both the partially sighted and the blind (particularly with the less intelligent and those suffering from additional handicaps), though there is as yet very little experience of this in this country. The place of programmed learning in schools for the visually handicapped and the production of suitable programmes should be the subject of further study (see Chapter 10).

7.30 If schools for the visually handicapped are to be equipped with a growing amount of equipment there will be an increasing need for competent technical support both to construct and to maintain the equipment and to undertake the routine production of material for use with it. All schools for the visually handicapped with any significant amount of equipment should employ at least one full-time technician for this work. This could be supplemented by the technical services of local education authorities.

7.31 We hope that local education authorities will make the whole range of their advisory services available to non-maintained special schools for the visually handicapped, equally with maintained schools. If schools can seek assistance from authorities' specialist advisers (for example in music, crafts and health education), it will help to keep them in touch with current educational thinking and practice. Schools should also be encouraged to make the fullest use of any other community or advisory resources, e.g. in music or drama, which could be relevant. Many of the Schools Council and Nuffield Project materials, e.g. in science and mathematics, have much which would be of value for teaching the visually handicapped.

7.32 *English Language and Literature* are basic to the education of any child, whether handicapped or not. We have already explained the difficulties which a visually handicapped child may experience in developing his language and vocabulary, and formal instruction in English at all stages of school has a major role to play here. But special attention should be given to ensuring that children understand the meaning of language and the reality to which it refers, to prevent the use of meaningless verbiage. English composition may be difficult for the child who cannot scan written work quickly, and more use should be made of tape recorders for oral composition. Every possible means should be employed of developing oral English. Drama has great value for both blind and partially sighted pupils: it can help to develop confidence, to improve posture, to encourage the use of appropriate gestures, and generally to make the pupil concentrate on movement and orientation.

7.33 *Mathematics* is a subject in which both blind and partially sighted children can achieve very high attainment, though calculation may be rather slow. Raised outline diagrams and three-dimensional models are needed in learning geometry, etc. Some of these are available from the RNIB and elsewhere, but many are devised by the teachers themselves. Here again, teachers would find it helpful to pool their experience, and courses arranged by HM Inspectorate provide an appropriate forum for this. Much useful information is also included in the publication, " The Teaching of Science and Mathematics to the Blind."[7] New methods of learning mathematics are helpful to all visually handicapped pupils, because they encourage investigation and discovery. Some of the new content depends more for its understanding on visual awareness than the older content which it has replaced, and special tactile material may need to be prepared in consequence.

7.34 *The Natural Sciences* can give rise to great difficulties for visually handicapped pupils, because they are subjects which rely heavily on demonstration and practical work. Nevertheless, science teaching should be a sine qua non in all schools for the visually handicapped. As is apparent from " The Teaching of Science and Mathematics to the Blind," a number of instruments and devices has been designed which can be employed for practical work particularly in physics. It is now possible to convert instrument scales into digital readings,

---

[7] Report to the Viscount Nuffield Auxiliary Fund, 1970, available from the RNIB.

and as many adaptations of this kind as possible should be made available. In biology, large-scale models, especially of the structure of the body, are valuable to supplement studies of the real subjects. Practical work in chemistry is less easy since this relies so greatly on the visual perception of changes in colour, etc. The ecological studies of rural science may afford great possibilities. Though blind students should as far as possible use normal apparatus, further investigation is required into the design and adaptation of instruments and into the best methods of teaching science to the blind at all age-levels and throughout the range of ability (see Chapter 10).

7.35 In some schools for the partially sighted, the teaching of science is very similar to that in ordinary schools but in others it is quite inadequate and occasionally non-existent, because qualified teachers and suitable equipment are unavailable. Provision for teaching science should be reviewed at an early opportunity by the schools. Where there are only one or two pupils in a small school wishing to pursue science to examination level, provision of equipment and apparatus for them would obviously be expensive. In such circumstances, arrangements could and should be made for the children to attend a nearby sighted school, with specialist help for the necessary individual science tuition.

7.36 In teaching *Foreign Languages* to visually handicapped children, one of the main problems is the shortage of books for blind children referred to in paragraphs 7.17 and 7.18. There are also some difficulties over braille contractions in foreign languages. Despite these difficulties, both blind and partially sighted children can do well at languages. Language laboratories are of course particularly valuable in teaching visually handicapped children, and are employed by some schools. There is also some shortage of specialist language teachers, which arises partly because many of the schools for the visually handicapped are very small. Consideration should, however, be given in these circumstances to enabling the small numbers of children with particular aptitude for languages to attend sighted schools part-time. Alternatively, the special schools should be given the opportunity of recruiting part-time language teachers. The few schools that teach classical languages report no particular difficulties with them.

7.37 *Geography* is a subject presenting a great difficulty for visually handicapped children, because modern methods of teaching, geared to the needs of sighted children, depend increasingly on visual aids such as maps, diagrams and slides. Special methods are required in presenting maps and abstracting details for the partially sighted. Embossed maps are produced for the blind, but the amount of detailed information they can convey is limited, and they can be extremely confusing. Further investigation is required into the most suitable type of thermoform production and the use of this medium in teaching. Schools should make the greatest possible use of models to supply information and to maintain interest. Field work and visits to geological and natural history museums can also be of great value, and schools should increasingly look outside the classroom in determining the content of the geography curriculum.

7.38 *History* has some of the disadvantages of geography for the visually handicapped, particularly in so far as it relies on visual aids. For blind children, there is, however, the additional difficulty imposed by the need to make con-

F

stant reference to standard works, which is not easily achieved in braille. A similar difficulty is encountered by partially sighted children, who cannot scan a printed page quickly. This problem can to a certain degree be solved by the use of tape-recorded material and summarising techniques.

7.39 *Social Studies* are a particularly important curriculum item for visually handicapped children, who are often less well informed about current affairs than sighted children because they cannot—either at all or with ease—read newspapers and periodicals. Blind children can make use of the RNIB's abstract of the news for braille readers, but both blind and partially sighted children need to be stimulated by informal study of broadcast news and talks. Visits to local courts or to meetings of the local council can enliven social studies for the visually handicapped. There is really no reason why parties of visually handicapped children, with suitable preparation, should not visit all the places commonly visited by sighted children as part of their social studies programmes. At the present time schools for the visually handicapped do not appear to give social studies the attention they deserve, and their coverage of them should be extended. In boarding schools, this could well be achieved informally in the evenings.

7.40 In *Religious and Moral Education* there have been radical changes over the last few years in both ordinary and special schools. Opportunities are often now provided for fully participant discussion of religious and moral questions of all kinds in what might be termed an open-ended search for truth. Schools for the blind and for the partially sighted which have not already done so should adopt this new approach, since it encourages the pupils themselves to bring up and explore together with their teacher topics arising from their own particular circumstances as visually handicapped young people.

7.41 Schools can obtain considerable help in developing a new approach from the new Agreed Syllabuses, from additional notes on religious education published by Cambridgeshire and Hampshire, from the Durham Report and from the Report of the Social Morality Council. The report of a Scottish committee on moral and religious education in Scottish schools was published in March, 1972.

7.42 *Music* offers great possibilities for visually handicapped children since it is a subject in which they are less seriously disadvantaged than in many others when compared with sighted people. Most schools for the blind and the partially sighted place great stress on music, and give their pupils every opportunity for singing, instrumental playing and musical appreciation. Many of them use part-time specialist teachers to instruct in the playing of the less common instruments. Music should occupy a major place in all schools for the visually handicapped, but further investigation is required of the best methods of teaching it (see Chapter 10). Every school should have properly sound-proofed music rooms, even if it has only junior pupils. A wide variety of instruments should be available and should be maintained at a high standard. The teaching of musical appreciation and the study of musical form and simple musical composition should be extended. Musical notation can be transcribed in braille, but it is difficult and cumbersome to read and would be of use only to those with a special interest in music. However, blind children who cannot read it can still achieve high instrumental standards and can take part in ensemble playing. The provision of music in larger format, and the use of fixed low visual aids and overhead projection, are of value to partially sighted children.

7.43 *Arts and Crafts* are already very well established in schools for the visually handicapped, most of which offer a very wide range of subjects. All arts and crafts are of immense value in encouraging children to develop their tactile perception and the potential for creative achievement even among totally blind children and those with very little residual vision is quite remarkable. Even where lack of vision prevents a child from approaching the standards of sighted children (for example in painting), he may derive a great deal of satisfaction from trying his hand and should not be discouraged from attempting any arts and crafts which appeal to him. Activities such as sculpture, pottery, woodwork and all types of craft work can greatly build up the confidence of a visually handicapped child, and the end result may give a far greater sense of achievement than it would to a sighted child. The aim should never be merely to copy the productions of sighted people. The results of craft work may also be valuable in giving the child's teacher an indication of his employment potential. Some craft work of course involves potential dangers for the visually handicapped child, with such pieces of equipment as chisels, pottery kilns and lathes; nevertheless, with proper precautions and adequate standards of safety, the visually handicapped child can generally do much the same kind of work as would a sighted child.

7.44 Instruction in *Typewriting* geared to *Commercial Studies* is offered by many schools. We have already referred in paragraphs 7.10 and 7.14 to the value of typewriting for visually handicapped children who find handwriting very difficult. For commercial studies typing layout and tabulation are of greater importance, and the difficulties in teaching them to blind children can be overcome. Children with sufficient residual vision can be instructed in copy-typing. It is however important for them to use a stand or other device for the copy material, so that they do not have constantly to bend over the desk to read it but can easily turn from it to the typewriter and back again. Audio-typing is particularly suitable for visually handicapped children.

7.45 *Home Economics and Domestic Science* are extremely important subjects for visually handicapped children of both sexes. Children have very often been completely sheltered in the home environment, and without considerable help at school will be ill-equipped to leave home and take their place in the sighted world. There is an enormous amount that the visually handicapped child has to learn, including the safe use of cooking and laundry equipment and of common smaller items of kitchen equipment, the differentiation of similar cooking ingredients, the methodical storage of household material to avoid confusion, and simple hand-sewing and the use of a sewing machine. A detailed and systematic curricular approach is therefore necessary. This applies equally to domestic science and to other aspects of home management such as the balancing of the household budget. In laying out a room for teaching domestic science schools should pay particular attention to the sensible placing of temperature gauges and careful general layout of furniture and equipment.

7.46 *Health Education* is extremely important for visually handicapped children. According to their evidence, all schools for the visually handicapped lay stress upon hygiene and the care of clothes and of the person, often as the opportunity arises during lessons in biology, home economics or physical education. An ad hoc approach is unsatisfactory and a structured programme is needed which, in schools with residential accommodation, must involve the child care staff as well as the teaching staff.

7.47 *Sex Education* is an important part of health education, but some schools for the visually handicapped treat it somewhat more hesitantly than they treat, for example, hygiene. A recent survey by Dr Langdon showed that about 90% of parents of blind children think sex education should be covered in schools at the secondary stage, though many fewer favour sex education at the primary stage. However, only about a quarter of the children surveyed stated that they had in fact received any sex education at all at school.

7.48 We have received evidence to the effect that many blind children are at a comparatively late stage ignorant not only of the biological details of the reproductive process but even of the basic differences between the sexes and of sexual response. Sex education for the blind is therefore a specialised task, requiring skilled and experienced instruction; in our view it should be the responsibility of the schools, in close co-operation with parents. We doubt the benefits of systematic sex education at the primary stage. Good relationships in the primary school years and the sensible answering of children's questions are however essential; and the curriculum ought to provide for the imparting of the necessary information.

7.49 At the secondary stage, however, a positive policy for and programme of sex education becomes essential for all visually handicapped children. Some opportunities for it will arise naturally during ordinary biology lessons, but schools will need to set aside some time specifically for a formal treatment of the subject. Excellent plastic models are now available for demonstration. Basic genetics should be included towards the end of the course so that the genetic counselling we discussed in Chapter 3 will be understood by the children in the light of what they have learnt in the classroom situation. For the visually handicapped as for ordinary children, education in the facts of sex must of course go hand in hand with opportunities to discuss the moral implications of those facts.

PHYSICAL EDUCATION, INCLUDING TRAINING IN MOBILITY, POSTURE AND THE ELIMINATION OF MANNERISMS

7.50 Although the range of physical activities is restricted in some schools for the visually handicapped, it is commendably wide in most. We regard games and sports and other forms of physical education as of great importance in relation to the full development of the natural physique, to mobility training and to the gaining of general physical confidence. Swimming is of particular value, since water is an element in which blind children can move with relative ease. All schools should either possess their own swimming pool or have a learner's pool and enjoy easy access to a full-size one.

7.51 There is, however, one general aspect of physical education about which there is some argument and which merits attention as a separate issue. It has been suggested to us in evidence that the physical activities of partially sighted children must be restricted because some of the children suffer from vision defects which are liable to sudden deterioration as a result of sharp blows or knocks. This was the view generally held at one time. Current ophthalmic opinion is that, except in very rare cases, there is no need to prevent any visually handicapped children from participating in physical activities which they would enjoy and which could be of benefit to them. Accordingly, we take the view that, even though it may cause some difficulties, a division has to be made between those who can safely indulge in physical exercise of various kinds and the very small number who cannot. Although greater safety precautions must be taken than for sighted children and many games will need some adaptation before they are suitable for the visually handicapped, all blind and partially sighted children should be encouraged to take part in all forms of physical education which they can enjoy without risk. In some sports and games they will be able to play against sighted children without being too seriously disadvantaged by their visual handicap.

7.52 Training in mobility (see Appendix H), in posture and in the elimination of mannerisms is a central feature of physical education for the visually handicapped. If the visually handicapped person is to play the fullest possible part in the community at large, it is vital that he should be as physically independent as he can within the bounds of safety, and free from avoidable mannerisms and posture defects, which otherwise tend to draw undue attention to him. The latter are of course liable to affect health also. Dr Fine's survey of children in schools for the blind and partially sighted gave an indication of the prevalence of mannerisms and poor mobility. Of the children surveyed, 9·6% of the partially sighted and 45% of the blind displayed one or more mannerisms; 4·5% of the partially sighted and 25% of the blind had poor mobility which could not be ascribed to physical handicap. There seemed to be some correlation between high intelligence and good mobility and the absence of mannerisms. Although the problems of blind children were predictably worse than those of the partially sighted, the percentages of partially sighted children affected by mannerisms and poor mobility were by no means insignificant. The survey's figures, however, for both blind and partially sighted children no doubt understate the scale of the training problem for the schools, since many of the older children would already have responded to mobility training by the time Dr Fine saw them.

7.53 The blind child in particular needs careful instruction to encourage confidence in the movements of his own body in relation to animate and inanimate objects around him. He must also learn how to hold his body (in particular, his head and hands) and the importance of appropriate gesture in communication. All too often, the blind child has had inadequate opportunities for developing independence and mobility; the development of good posture and the avoidance of mannerisms might be assisted by a more normal range of activity in the pre-school years.

7.54 According to their evidence, all schools for the blind give some kind of mobility training, though there are variations in the time allotted to it, the methods of instruction and staff employed on it. The Long Cane is widely used as an aid to independent mobility. Some schools have detailed programmes of instruction under the control of a full-time instructor qualified in mobility training, and they try to ensure that all teachers and house staff are acquainted with the basic principles of mobility training. It is essential that mobility training for all children of adequate intelligence should include the use of raised maps and the recognition of environmental features (through touch and hearing); it should also cover training in the ability to judge distance by means of reflection of sounds (echolocation). The children should acquire the ability to explore unfamiliar environments as well as a knowledge of their familiar surroundings. They also need to learn how to use public transport. A systematic programme of skilled mobility training is essential in all schools for the blind, and there should be the equivalent of at least one full-time qualified mobility instructor who should be responsible for the school's programme of mobility training and for instructing other members of staff in the basic principles. As many members of staff as possible should also attend short courses. at the National Mobility Centre. The larger schools for the blind will probably need more than one mobility instructor, for, although some mobility instruction can be given to children in groups, a substantial part of any mobility programme will require instruction on a 1 : 1 basis.

7.55 From Dr Fine's survey it appears that a considerable number of partially sighted children may need as much encouragement in developing independent mobility as do children in schools for the blind; and a systematic approach to their training is no less necessary (for further discussion see Appendix H, Section B). It is unfortunate that at present many partially sighted children do not have the benefit of a systematic programme.

7.56 Formal programmes of mobility training can be complemented by other parts of the curriculum. We have already spoken of the contribution which physical activities can make. Visits outside the school (which we have mentioned as valuable in widening a child's environmental experience) also can build confidence and, more important, can greatly stimulate in a visually handicapped child the desire to explore independently. In order to secure consistency of approach between school and home, schools should do their utmost through discussions with parents to ensure that they understand the importance to children of wide experience of the environment. It is desirable as well that school mobility instructors should maintain close liaison with the families so that those children who would benefit from mobility training during the holidays can receive it.

LEISURE ACTIVITIES

7.57 Schools for the visually handicapped encourage a wide range of leisure activities, though they are better able to do this for boarding pupils. We particularly commend the arrangements that are made for visually handicapped children to mix with sighted children in school clubs (both in the special schools themselves and in neighbouring ordinary schools) and in organisations for boys and girls in the neighbourhood. Visits to the homes of sighted children are of great value for blind children if these can be arranged.

7.58 Day pupils present more difficulties for the schools: many of them have some way to travel and use special transport leaving at a given time each day. Furthermore parents are often understandably reluctant to allow visually handicapped children to remain at school after the end of the normal school day. These children, however, have no less need of varied and stimulating leisure pursuits than boarding pupils. We suggest that local authority social work staff (who should have information about all visually handicapped children living in their areas) should make special efforts to see that these children are involved in outside activities as much as possible.

THE PLACE OF PUBLIC EXAMINATIONS

7.59 Many visually handicapped children possess the ability to take public examinations open to sighted children, and the results they achieve are often impressive The examinations taken cover an average spread of subjects at GCE ' A ' and ' O ' levels and CSE (see paragraph 5.64). All the evidence which we have received suggests that the opportunity to take public examinations is extremely valuable for the visually handicapped, both in building up a child's confidence in his ability to take his place in the sighted world and also in demonstrating to potential employers a child's capacities despite his visual handicap.

7.60 Schools for both the blind and partially sighted seem somewhat reluctant to employ CSE Mode III, which involves assessment by the school based on a syllabus designed to suit the school's requirements. There may be some fear either that Mode III is of a lower standard than other Modes or that potential employers and others will believe that special allowances have been made in the standard required of handicapped pupils. These fears are mistaken, since external moderators ensure that standards are high. We recommend that all visually handicapped schools with pupils up to 16 should provide CSE courses over a reasonable range of subjects for as many pupils as possible, with the use if necessary of specialist facilities in neighbouring secondary schools for sighted children, and that they should consider carefully the advantages of adopting Mode III.

7.61 Whatever examination is taken, visually handicapped pupils will almost certainly be at some disadvantage in the time it takes them to read questions and to set down the answers. With the agreement of examining boards, visually handicapped pupils are often allowed more time to complete the papers than sighted children; and they may also be allowed alternative methods for recording their answers. When needed, these practices should be adopted in all examinations for the visually handicapped.

RECOMMENDATIONS

7.62 This chapter contains a large number of general comments and detailed suggestions. Some of the most important specific points have been picked out in the next paragraph as recommendations (apart from requirements for research, which will be summarised in Chapter 10). They need however to be read in their context; and we hope that attention will also be paid to the other points made in the course of the chapter.

7.63 We recommend that:

(1) blind children should possess their own Perkins brailler and should retain it when they leave school (paragraph 7.09);

(2) all visually handicapped children who can benefit from it should be taught to type and they should be provided with their own typewriter when they leave school (paragraphs 7.10 and 7.14);

(3) staffing should be sufficiently generous to allow periods of individual teaching for partially sighted children with special difficulties in learning to read (paragraph 7.11);

(4) schools for the blind should have braille reproduction equipment. Schools for the partially sighted should have access to an enlarger and to offset litho copying equipment. Technicians should be available for the operation and maintenance of all apparatus and equipment (paragraphs 7.16, 7.18 and 7.30);

(5) the appropriate Government departments should take urgent steps to ensure that the production of books, including recorded books, for visually handicapped children is fully adequate (paragraphs 7.19 and 7.23);

(6) tape recorders and talking books should be available for all visually handicapped children, who should be instructed in their use. If possible, they should have their own cassette tape recorders on leaving school (paragraphs 7.21 and 7.23);

(7) schools for the partially sighted should be equipped with low visual aids for individual children and audio-visual aids. There should be good general lighting and an adjustable system of individual lighting (paragraphs 7.12, 7.25, 7.26 and 7.28);

(8) local education authorities should make their advisory services available to non-maintained special schools, who should also make use of any other community or advisory resources (paragraph 7.31);

(9) consideration should be given to improving the methods of teaching certain subjects, especially the natural sciences (paragraphs 7.32–7.49);

(10) all visually handicapped children should be encouraged to take part in all forms of physical education which they can enjoy without risk (paragraph 7.51);

(11) a systematic programme of mobility training should be provided for all partially sighted children who need it, as well as for all blind children (paragraph 7.55); and

(12) all schools for the visually handicapped containing pupils of secondary age should enable as many as possible to take courses for public examinations, including CSE. They should consider adopting CSE Mode III (paragraph 7.60).

CHAPTER 8 : FURTHER EDUCATION, HIGHER EDUCATION AND VOCATIONAL GUIDANCE

INTRODUCTION

8.01 For visually handicapped pupils who attend special schools the minimum school leaving age is 16. The pupil who is approaching this age has a number of decisions to make for which he requires guidance. These include whether to continue education beyond the leaving age; if so, whether to do it by a course in school or at a college of further education; whether to opt to go into employment; and, if so, how to find out what sorts of jobs are suited to him and obtain the appropriate training.

8.02 The body of this chapter is divided into two sections–one on vocational guidance and assessment and the other on further education and training. The two centres, however, to which blind school leavers may go for vocational guidance and assessment, Hethersett Centre at Reigate in Surrey and Queen Alexandra College at Harborne, Birmingham, also provide facilities for social adjustment and continued general education. It seems desirable to deal with the two centres as a whole, and so all their functions will be considered in the section on vocational guidance and assessment.

VOCATIONAL GUIDANCE AND ASSESSMENT

The present position

8.03 The 2 centres at Hethersett and Harborne include among their aims bridging the gap between school and employment. In January 1971 Hethersett had 42 students on roll and Harborne 49. Full-time vocational training is given only at Harborne, where 16 selected students (usually men) take a training course in light engineering after completing the assessment course. The length of time which students spend at these centres varies, but is usually from 2 to 6 terms. On leaving, students are recommended either for employment or for further education or training, and the centres' employment officers follow up their subsequent progress. About a quarter of the intake to the centres comes from schools other than special schools for the blind. Partially sighted students —some of whom may have already spent an unsuccessful period in employment —are able to attend provided that, on their Forms BD8, Section C (4) is endorsed to the effect that they are likely soon to become blind or have such a visual defect that they would benefit from training for employment or from other services appropriate for blind people.

8.04 There is no equivalent of Harborne or Hethersett specifically for partially sighted school leavers, but if these have adequate residual vision Industrial Rehabilitation Units (IRUs) sometimes help by providing places for a few students above compulsory school age on short assessment courses, and, exceptionally, on young persons' work preparation courses. Some schools occasionally send pupils of average and below average ability to IRUs for short courses designed to assess in an industrial situation the potential for work of boys and girls with any handicap; these courses last from 5–10 days. The provision of short assessment courses depends upon the availability of an occupational psychologist. The work preparation courses take all types of handicapped school leaver and combine education, vocational assessment and work preparation. These courses last for one school term with the possibility of extension for a second term.

Evidence received

8.05 The questionnaires sent to schools by our working parties on curricula for the blind and for the partially sighted asked about arrangements for vocational guidance. The replies revealed a great diversity of practice. Some schools began consideration of their pupils' futures at the age of 14 or 15 and assembled panels to consider each case. Panel membership varied: the local careers officer, the head teacher, a careers teacher, the Blind Persons Resettlement Officer, the RNIB Employment Officer and (more rarely) the school medical officer were mentioned as members. Some schools for the blind considered that guidance was primarily a matter for the assessment centres and did not attempt case conferences. Boarding schools described various means of getting in touch with careers officers in the areas of the pupils' homes. Some relied on their local careers officer to make contact with his counterpart in the home area, while others sent reports of case conferences to the home local authority; only rarely did the careers officer from the home authority visit the school. Evidence received other than from the schools stressed the need for close co-operation between the schools and the Youth Employment Service, and the need for a wider field of employment for the visually handicapped.

8.06 Most of the schools supplemented this formal guidance with talks by outside speakers and visits to places of further education and employment. Sometimes the curriculum for pupils in their last year or two was organised as a school leavers course. One school for the partially sighted described such a course: the syllabus included discussion of wages and deductions from them, training, apprenticeships and safety regulations, and visits to factories of various kinds, spare-time activities and the development of social relationships. Students on this course joined with others from nearby schools for the physically handicapped and delicate for a two-day session in which they had practice interviews with local employers. After hearing the employers' comments they were able to approach real interviews with more skill and confidence. Some of the schools for the blind also had school leavers' courses, often started for the benefit of students who were waiting to take up a place at one of the vocational assessment centres.

8.07 Some schools for the partially sighted considered that their pupils needed assessment centres similar to those at Harborne and Hethersett. Many witnesses from outside the schools also expressed this view.

Consideration of the issues

8.08 In our view careers guidance should begin at least 2 or 3 years before the pupil leaves school. We consider that for every visually handicapped pupil a case conference should be held by a team of experts which should maintain liaison with the pupil's comprehensive assessment team. The use of a team approach in vocational guidance for the handicapped pupil was in fact recommended to local education authorities by the DES in Circular 9/66. The composition of the team will vary with the needs of the pupil, but it should always include the careers officer and we hope that officers who specialise in the placement of handicapped young people will increase in number. In any event, the Disablement Resettlement Officer of the Department of Employment may be able to give helpful advice, and close liaison should be maintained with him. In appropriate cases the employment officers of vocational assessment centres should also be consulted. We believe that special schools would do well to designate an assistant teacher to help the headteacher with the organisation and content of careers education in school and to assist in careers advisory work with outside bodies. Those teachers concerned with careers guidance should be encouraged to go on courses of special training and be given time in school hours for their work. Pupils who are likely to continue their studies after school will also benefit from vocational guidance. Although the choice of subjects to be studied is relevant to the opportunities of future employment, a broad education is needed which might lead to a widening of the opportunities of employment of the visually handicapped and which would be valuable for leisure pursuits.

8.09 In the case of pupils who go to boarding schools, the importance of effective liaison with the careers officer in the pupil's home area, as well as with parents, cannot be too strongly emphasised. After a preliminary assessment of a pupil's capabilities has been made, the careers officer in the school area should be responsible for getting in touch with the home area careers officer, who should then review job prospects. The home area careers officer should see the young person and his or her parents during school holidays, starting well before the school leaving date, and take appropriate action if placement in employment is required. It may seem expensive in staff time, but much wasted effort and frustration will be avoided if the school careers officer is able to ensure that the advice given to the pupils is in accordance with the employment prospects in the home area. Whatever administrative arrangements are made for careers guidance, it is important that the pupil's own wishes should be given serious consideration.

8.10 Preparation for leaving school must be aimed, especially during the last year at school, at bridging the gap between school and the outside world. One of the most important aims of a school leavers' course is the preparation of the visually handicapped young person for the change from the narrow world of a special school, with its familiar pattern of relationships and its readier understanding of visual disability, to the broader life of the community in which he will have to fend for himself. Many of the features of the course at the particular school that we described in paragraph 8.06 are relevant to this theme. It is also of the first importance that pupils should be helped to come to terms with their handicap in relation to the employment situation. We believe that the emphasis in such courses should be not so much on narrowly vocational or pre-vocational training as on an increasing competence in the basic skills such as mathematics and English and in developing independent mobility. During their working lives many people including the visually handicapped may have to learn to adapt to a variety of occupations, which will be easier if they have the grounding of a sound general education, social maturity and an ability to work with other people. Subjects should be taught in a way which relates them to post-school experience, and the 15-year-old may be better served by versatility than by specialisation.

8.11 A few pupils who are rightly educated in schools for the partially sighted find it difficult or impossible to earn their living at work involving the use of sight. This may be because their vision is seriously impaired or deteriorating, or because the visual requirements of school and work are different; thus it would be dangerous to keep one's eyes as close to a machine as to a book. In the evidence we received there was criticism that some schools for the partially sighted do too little to instruct these young people in the tactile methods which they may have to rely on at work. We believe that the reason for this may be that the problem is recognised too late; often the question whether it is necessary to complete Section C(4) on Form BD8 is considered only when the pupil is about to leave school, whereas it should first be considered 2 or 3 years earlier. Once the problem is recognised, it will need tactful handling on the part of the school, especially since schools for the partially sighted rightly put great emphasis on the use of available vision. For this reason we do not think it practicable to lay down any general rules as to when and how such instruction should be given. Because a partially sighted person needs, for example, to learn to read a braille micrometer, it does not necessarily mean that he has to learn braille symbols for general reading purposes. The assessment team responsible for filling out Form BD8 (or its replacement) when a child leaves school should, as a matter of course, receive feed-back information from the careers officer about his subsequent progress, since this might indicate a need to amend the certificate.

8.12 We believe that no blind child should go straight into employment at the age of 16, and that there should be adequate provision for all to continue in full-time education, assessment and possibly training, either at school or some other establishment, until they are at least 17. When they leave school, many blind pupils will need to go to a vocational assessment centre. We share the concern expressed to us by many of the head teachers of schools for the blind and by the Principal of Hethersett about the period of waiting (often up to 2 years) between application for a place at a vocational assessment centre and admission. It does not necessarily mean that during this period the boys and girls lack opportunities for purposeful study; the majority remain at school, and provided that it is possible for this school to provide an imaginative programme of work, and for the students to maintain a constructive attitude to work while still in a school setting, the period can be put to good use in furthering general education. Indeed one school had found it so useful that it recommended that the school leaving age for blind pupils should be raised to 17. But for most of these young people the school environment is not really suitable; and the present delay in admission to the assessment centres must not continue.

8.13 We have considered whether it is advisable to enlarge the assessment centres; and whether there should be any changes in the functions and curriculum of Hethersett and Harborne. Having noted that the number of blind pupils in

84

schools has been decreasing since the period when retrolental fibroplasia caused such a sudden increase in visual defects, we do not consider that the centres as at present organised should be enlarged. They are however still seeking to carry out their original aims, as outlined in the Report of the Working Party on the Employment of Blind Persons (1951), namely vocational guidance, social adjustment and continued general education. It seems to us very questionable whether these 3 functions can still be combined in one centre, particularly with the increasing number of more handicapped and backward students now requiring admission. The latter can certainly benefit from opportunities for social adjustment, but perhaps only to a minimal extent from vocational guidance and continued education; and their prolonged attendance in the centres can only delay the admission of those whose primary need is assessment. Accordingly, we believe that serious consideration ought to be given to the fundamental reorganisation of the centres' functions and curriculum, and full advantage should be taken of any relevant provision for the sighted.

8.14 Several points have occurred to us about the methods of assessment employed at Hethersett and Harborne. We noted that, while students obtained some actual work experience outside the centres, one of the main features of the curriculum was to introduce the students to a number of tasks associated with various commercial and industrial occupations (such as machine operating, assembly, packing, telephony, typing, etc.). The intention was to give them rudimentary knowledge of what is involved in these occupations, and to assess their practical potential and personal qualities. No objective study has been made of the extent to which these practised tasks are, in fact, a true guide to occupational potential or provide genuine work experience; and they should be made the subject of a research study by an occupational psychologist to ascertain whether any changes should be introduced into methods of assessment (see Chapter 10). In addition, assessment should have regard to any enquiries being carried out by the Department of Employment or other agencies into new areas of employment for the blind. There might also be a thorough investigation of the specific abilities and disabilities of visually handicapped workers, and of the extent to which new methods of training might be related to these and to the opportunities for employment.

8.15 Blind young people who also have mental, behavioural or physical handicaps present special problems. If the additional handicap is not severe they may be able to proceed to vocational assessment and training but, as stated above, we are aware that for the majority the existing assessment facilities are not suitable. Nevertheless we consider that many of them could benefit from a further opportunity for social training and maturation, away from the environment of school, and before any more permanent placement is made. The more socially acceptable they can become, the better chance they have of being absorbed into the community. We consider that there should be a residential centre, serving the whole country, whose programme is designed to meet the needs of these youngsters. The content of courses might well be similar to work schemes developed for the less able senior children in sighted schools. From the residential centre, a few young people would proceed into employment (which would usually be sheltered) but the majority would need to go to adult training centres or, if unsuitable for these, into residential care. We envisage most of those in adult training centres living at home, with the remainder accommodated in hostels attached to selected centres. Where training centres contain visually handicapped youngsters, special schools in the neighbourhood should if possible make expert advice and services available. The present provision for those who need residential care is inadequate; this seems to us to be a field to which a voluntary body might well turn its attention.

8.16 We strongly endorse the view of many schools for the partially sighted that the absence of any vocational assessment centre for the partially sighted is one of the most serious deficiencies in provision for the visually handicapped. There are however several possible ways of meeting this need. We have considered whether Harborne and Hethersett themselves could take more partially sighted students other than those certified as having so little vision that they will have to work by blind methods. A disadvantage of this would be that the abilities and employment opportunities of the partially sighted are very different from those of the blind, and the centres would have to be varied considerably to take in any significant number of partially sighted students. We can see no substantial benefits to weigh against these disadvantages and have thus concluded that this would not be a sensible solution.

8.17 The alternative is to establish one or more new centres for vocational assessment of the partially sighted, perhaps linked in some way with the IRUs. Before any conclusions could be reached as to how in detail this should be achieved, there would need to be a national investigation of employment opportunities for the partially sighted and research into appropriate methods of assessing suitability for them. We recommend that the whole question of vocational assessment and employment for the partially sighted should be the subject of further study as a matter of urgency (see Chapter 10). The main questions to be answered are:

    (i) how many of the partially sighted are likely to find difficulty in obtaining employment?

    (ii) what kinds of employment are particularly suited to the partially sighted?

    (iii) how can suitability for such employment best be assessed?

    (iv) do only those with the most severe visual defects or multiple handicaps need an extended assessment?

    (v) could the need for vocational assessment of the partially sighted best be met by a single assessment centre or by a number of separate, or linked centres?

    (vi) how should the activities of an assessment centre be co-ordinated with the work of the IRUs?

    (vii) where should such a centre or centres be set up and by whom?

FURTHER EDUCATION AND TRAINING

Present position

8.18 The more academically gifted of the visually handicapped pupils aim, like their sighted contemporaries, at achieving passes at the Ordinary and Advanced

Levels of the General Certificate of Education. They may do this at one of the selective schools or in certain cases at non-selective schools, sometimes going out to schools for the sighted or to colleges of further education for tuition in certain subjects. A few leave the schools after GCE Ordinary Levels and proceed to sixth form work at sighted schools or colleges of further education in their home area. Some blind students take a more vocationally orientated course of further education at the Royal Normal College, going there straight from school or after a period at a vocational assessment centre.

8.19 Further education and vocational training are provided specially for blind students in the following ways:

(i) The Royal Normal College offers courses in commerce, piano tuning, and music for suitable candidates; it also has a broadly based curriculum of further education, including considerable training in mobility. The courses vary in length according to the ability of the student and his or her standard of work on arrival. Piano technicians are trained in three years or less; shorthand and audio-typists need on average a ten term course. Younger students entering the College usually follow a year's course consisting of 50% typing with attendant skills and 50% further education and essential training for the blind, including mobility; the time spent on vocational training increases after this basic year. Some students find it best to start the vocational training full-time straight away; these students are usually the older ones.

(ii) The RNIB has a residential training college in London for blind shorthand and audio-typists and telephonists. The typing courses last about a year or 9 months and the telephony course 3-5 months. The RNIB also maintains in London a school of physiotherapy for blind students, with an associated hostel. The course, which lasts 3 years, conforms fully to the requirements of the Chartered Society of Physiotherapy by which it is recognised.

(iii) The Government Training Centre at Letchworth has an 8-week training course in machine-operating, inspection, the use of Braille precision instruments and repetitive assembly work. Hostel accommodation is provided.

(iv) In certain circumstances the Department of Employment pays fees and maintenance grants for blind students on other courses. Computer programming has proved a suitable occupation for blind people and special arrangements have been made for them to take appropriate courses.

8.20 The partially sighted have no equivalent of the Royal Normal College for further education, though some of them (chiefly those who also have physical handicaps) go on to establishments such as Queen Elizabeth's College or St. Loyes College, which are primarily intended for the physically handicapped. There is also a course in audio-typing for the partially sighted at Kingsway College of Further Education in London.

8.21 The position about the grants and help with expenses available is rather complicated. Local education authority awards to visually handicapped students on courses of higher education are made on the same basis as those for sighted students, but authorities normally use their discretionary powers to be as generous as possible to handicapped students. Again like sighted students, visually handicapped students at colleges of further education may receive a grant at the discretion of their local education authority. Students at the Royal Normal College on further education courses usually have their fees paid by their local education authorities and also receive pocket money (though older students who may exceptionally be placed at the RNC by the Department of Employment for training in piano-tuning receive grants direct from that Department). For visually handicapped full-time students who need equipment and services the RNIB may currently make an initial grant of up to £200. These extra expenses may include: the cost of braillers, typewriters, tape-recorders, tapes and, where voluntary assistance is not sufficient, the cost of having books read. Transport is also liable to be more expensive. At the same time the visually handicapped student is much less likely than the sighted to be able to find a vacation job.

Evidence received

8.22 Most of the evidence received expressed the view that visually handicapped students should be integrated with sighted students for further and higher education. Students however should be helped financially with the provision of books and equipment, and colleges and staff in further education should be made aware of the needs of these students. The services which the RNIB already operates should be developed.

Consideration of the issues

8.23 For some blind and many partially sighted school leavers, integration in existing further education establishments for the sighted may be preferable to a special institution for the visually handicapped. The polytechnics and colleges of further education provide rich educational, technical, cultural and social opportunities. Though it must be said that the admission of visually handicapped students can make considerable demands on such establishments for the sighted, many of the difficulties of assimilation can be avoided by careful advance planning. In London, for example, schools for the partially sighted have for several years had a scheme for part-time attendance of older pupils at local colleges of further education. Through careful liaison between the staffs of the special schools and the colleges, this has proved very valuable both in explaining the needs of partially sighted students to further education staff and in overcoming the misgivings of students and individual teachers. Arrangements of this kind should be more widely instituted in other parts of the country. In addition there may be other pupils who would benefit on leaving school by taking a specific further education course for the visually handicapped to include mathematics, science, social and business studies. One such course could well be developed at the Royal Normal College, where a framework already exists which could be extended when the secondary school is discontinued (see paragraph 5.60).

8.24 Most universities and other higher education institutions now have experience of visually handicapped students and of their special needs, and experience has shown that many visually handicapped students are well able to hold their own without special educational provision at that stage. However, schools need to pay particular attention to preparing visually handicapped pupils for their student life, which will for many be the first time that they have attended full-time an educational institution primarily geared to meeting the needs of the sighted. Schools should ensure that all visually handicapped leavers proceeding to further and higher education are made known in advance to student medical and welfare services at those institutions. They should discuss both with the pupils and authorities concerned how their pupils can best be helped (both before and after leaving school) to make a successful transition from school to further and higher education. The RNIB has much experience in assisting blind students in higher education and is, in some cases, able to offer help to those in the partially sighted category. We believe, however, that the majority of partially sighted students need practical specialist help at this stage and that it is essential that both the students and those dealing with them should have access to consistent guidance and advice since many of their problems arise from ignorance of the degree and nature of the handicap and the misunderstandings which occur in consequence. We would hope, therefore, that the RNIB would be able to extend its supportive services in higher education to all visually handicapped students who need them.

8.25 Apart from attending universities or colleges the visually handicapped person who wishes to obtain higher qualifications can enrol on correspondence courses or with the Open University; for the blind students the RNIB provides supporting services. Although these forms of study have the disadvantage of providing at best a very limited contact between the visually handicapped student and the sighted student community, they will be appropriate in some cases and school leavers should be informed of these alternative opportunities.

8.26 As regards financial support, we consider that all visually handicapped students taking courses of higher and further education, whether at universities, colleges of further education, or at the Royal Normal College, Harborne or Hethersett, should (irrespective of help from other sources) be treated generously by local education authorities, so that the students' independence would be encouraged and they would be helped to prepare for life in the adult world. This makes it particularly desirable that students at the Royal Normal College, Harborne and Hethersett should receive some part at least of their maintenance grant direct.

8.27 There are many visually handicapped people of all ages who have left formal education, but who could benefit from attendance at evening classes or institutes. They may be slow to come forward because they feel that their presence in such classes will impose a burden on others or because they are reluctant to go out at night. The social workers who are in contact with them should explain the advantages of attendance and local education authorities should help with provision of facilities. In this way, the local authority may fulfil its duty under Section 2(c) of the Chronically Sick and Disabled Persons Act, 1970 to provide, where necessary, for the disabled person " lectures, games, outings or other recreational facilities outside his home or assistance to that person in taking advantage of educational facilities available to him." Occasionally the visually handicapped adults of an area may be able to get to-

G

gether for their own special classes; we learnt of cookery and horticulture classes for blind adults in certain areas. Again, the Open University and correspondence courses can provide valuable opportunities for the mature visually handicapped student, though they are subject to the disadvantage which we referred to in paragraph 8.25.

REGIONAL DISTRIBUTION

8.28 When the national plan for the education of the visually handicapped which we recommend in Chapter 6 is drawn up, the need should be considered for a more even distribution through the regions of the provision required for vocational guidance and assessment, further education and vocational training.

RECOMMENDATIONS

8.29 We recommend that:

(1) for each visually handicapped child careers guidance should begin at least 2 or 3 years before he leaves school, and for children in residential schools this guidance must be given in close consultation with the careers officers in the pupils' home areas, as well as with parents (paragraphs 8.08 and 8.09);

(2) for each visually handicapped child there should also be a careers case conference of a team of experts, in liaison with the child's comprehensive assessment team (paragraphs 8.08 and 8.09);

(3) the assessment team responsible for filling out Form BD8 (or its replacement) when a child leaves school should receive information from the careers officer about his subsequent progress, since this might indicate a need to amend the certificate (paragraph 8.11);

(4) no blind child should go straight into employment at the age of 16, but there should be additional provision for all to continue full-time education and/or training (whether at school or in some other establishment) until they are at least 17 years old (paragraph 8.12);

(5) the accommodation, functions and curriculum of the present assessment centres should be reviewed (paragraph 8.13);

(6) a residential centre should be established, serving the whole country, to provide social training for blind young people who have severe additional handicaps and are not likely to be suited to vocational assessment and training (paragraph 8.15);

(7) one or more centres should be established for the vocational assessment of the partially sighted, the number and form of which would depend on the results of research (paragraph 8.16);

(8) schemes for the part-time attendance at colleges of further education of visually handicapped pupils in their last years at school should be extended (paragraph 8.23);

(9) schools for the visually handicapped should maintain close liaison with further and higher education establishments for the sighted to facilitate their assimilation of visually handicapped students (paragraphs 8.23 and 8.24);

(10) local education authorities should grant-aid generously, irrespective of help from other sources, visually handicapped students taking courses at universities, colleges of further education and assessment centres (paragraph 8.26);

(11) more facilities should be provided by local education authorities for informal classes and activities in which visually handicapped adults can participate (paragraph 8.27);

(12) when the national plan for the education of the visually handicapped is drawn up, the need should be considered for a more even distribution through the regions of the provision required for vocational guidance and assessment, further education and vocational training (paragraph 8.28).

CHAPTER 9 : THE TRAINING OF TEACHERS AND RESIDENTIAL CHILD CARE STAFF

TEACHERS

The present position

9.01 At present the only special schools for handicapped pupils in which teachers are required to hold an additional qualification are those for the blind, the deaf and the partially hearing. Section 15(2) of the Handicapped Pupils and Special Schools Regulations, 1959 (as amended) laid down that all teachers in special schools should be qualified teachers, subject to certain exceptions, and empowered the Minister to prescribe further qualifications in respect of teachers of these three categories of children. The qualifications and the conditions required for obtaining them were restated in Appendix 4 to Circular 10/71 as follows:

" The Secretary of State requires teachers of blind ... children (except those engaged solely in teaching crafts, domestic or trade subjects, or other teachers as the Secretary of State may in exceptional circumstances decide) to have additional qualifications as indicated below. Those teaching at special schools must have the basic qualifications required for teachers in primary schools and must obtain one of the additional qualifications within three years of taking up a post.

Teachers in Schools for the Blind must either:

(a) obtain the School Teachers' Diploma of the College of Teachers of the Blind (obtained by studying while teaching in a special school)
or

(b) successfully complete the one-year course of training for teachers of the visually handicapped at Birmingham University (full-time study)."

" Teachers of classes or units for children who are blind in addition to being deaf or partially hearing (whether in a school for the blind or in one for the deaf or partially hearing) must have, or must obtain within three years (or such further period as the Secretary of State may in a particular case decide), one or other of the additional qualifications " laid down for teachers in schools for the blind or for teachers in schools for the deaf and partially hearing.

9.02 The School Teachers' Diploma of the College of Teachers of the Blind has existed for many years. The part-time course for the Diploma is a form of in-service training taken in combination with teaching in a school for the blind. Previous experience of teaching normal children is not required. The Diploma examination was described in evidence submitted to the Committee by the General Executive of the College of Teachers of the Blind:

92

" The Diploma Examination is based on the practical experience which a teacher gains in his first two years in a school. It tests his ability to read and write braille; it tests also his awareness of the problems and opportunities facing the teacher of blind children. Candidates, in addition, must offer a subject, or a combination of subjects, at a certain age range; a theory paper is then set on the teaching of this to blind children and examiners observe the candidate's teaching in his own school. The Board consists of practising teachers with long experience. Examination requirements are continually being altered to match the changing pattern of education in the schools and the varying needs of candidates. Payment is made by the Department (of Education and Science) to the CTB for the administration of the Diploma Examination. But the examiners do their work completely on a voluntary basis, receiving only expenses. This has always been a noteworthy feature of the administration of the examination."

9.03 The course at Birmingham University named in Circular 10/71 had its origin in the Fourth Report of the National Advisory Council on the Training and Supply of Teachers which was published in 1954. The Council recommended:

" One area training organisation or university department of education should be invited by the Ministry of Education to establish as soon as possible a one-year general course for teachers of handicapped children with special reference to teachers of the blind."

A number of changes has been made in the course over the years: in particular it now covers training for teaching both the blind and the partially sighted. Candidates for the course are expected to have had at least two years' teaching experience with normal children. Some additional experience in a school for blind or partially sighted children is regarded as desirable but not essential. The course gives practice in the teaching of blind and partially sighted children; a comprehensive general background of educational and developmental psychology; and study of the special needs of blind and partially sighted children and of the special methods of teaching and care required. Assessment for the award of the Supplementary Certificate for Teachers of Visually Handicapped Children[1] is based on practical work, a written examination and a dissertation on some topic related to the education of visually handicapped children. Students on this course also attend ' common core ' lectures with students who are studying to teach children with other handicaps and there is an extensive programme of visits to special schools of all kinds.

9.04 Anyone who is a qualified teacher may teach partially sighted children without obtaining a further qualification. Indeed, until the Birmingham course was extended to include training in the education of the partially sighted, there was no course of training specially provided for teachers of partially sighted pupils. In 1968–69 and 1969–70 students taking the Birmingham course could specialise in the education of the blind or of the partially sighted; 4 students elected to study the education of the partially sighted. As from 1970–71 all students train to teach both blind and partially sighted pupils; 8 started the

[1] From October, 1972 this will become the Diploma in the Education of the Visually Handicapped.

93

course in 1970 and 9 in 1971. A number of Colleges of Education and University Departments of Education provide general courses in the education of handicapped children and offer some guidance on the teaching of partially sighted children but this falls short of the intensive study of the methods of teaching these children which is provided by the Birmingham University course.

9.05 Surveys of teachers in visually handicapped schools showed that there were 33 full-time blind teachers in schools and further education establishments for the blind in 1969, and 2 visually handicapped teachers in schools for the partially sighted in 1970.

Evidence received

9.06 Many witnesses said that it was desirable for teachers intending to teach the visually handicapped to have some experience of teaching normal children before they entered special education.

9.07 The general tenor of the evidence which we received from teachers and other bodies about the School Teachers' Diploma of the College of Teachers of the Blind was critical, mainly because courses of this kind have certain disadvantages inseparable from in-service training. The young teacher's first years in special education were bound to impose something of a strain on him, and this was aggravated if he had to study in his spare time. Advice and guidance on the studies for the Diploma were supposed to be given by the head and more experienced members of the staff, but they were often too busy to spare sufficient time. Again it was very desirable for the young teacher to observe at some length the methods of educating the visually handicapped employed in schools other than his own, but it was difficult to second him for extended visits if he were a full-time member of the staff at his own school. On the other hand, few witnesses denied that a person of the requisite ability and personality could develop into a satisfactory teacher of the blind through the CTB qualification, and almost all agreed that some kind of provision for qualification through in-service training was necessary. One reason was that there was a number of persons (for example married women) who could give valuable service in the special schools, but who were not able to attend a course of full-time training for which the demand was too small to justify provision on a local basis. Secondly, where a teacher was a member of the staff of a residential school, it was difficult to get a replacement while he was away on the course.

9.08 We received little written evidence on the Birmingham course as such except from the University itself. A few people suggested that it was not sufficiently closely linked with current practice in the schools for the visually handicapped, or that it would be better for the course to be confined to theory and for the teaching practice to be taken in the subsequent year with the Certificate to be awarded on satisfactory completion. The extension of the course to cover the needs of partially sighted pupils was widely welcomed. A number of witnesses mentioned that there was sometimes difficulty in releasing a teacher for a year in order to undertake it. On the whole however head teachers seemed very favourably impressed with the quality of staff trained on this course. At the same time, some evidence pointed out that the teaching methods employed in schools for partially sighted were very different from those in schools for the blind. Accordingly, a training course might need to be longer than the present Birmingham course if it were to equip the teacher to teach both categories of children.

9.09 There was some disagreement among our witnesses about the desirability of training teachers of the partially sighted through general courses in special education. On the one hand, it was frequently said that the instruction so offered, though valuable as part of a general course, was not adequate as an introduction to modern methods of teaching the partially sighted. On the other hand, the point was made that, since so many partially sighted pupils suffered from additional handicaps, it was appropriate that the teachers' course should cover a variety of handicaps. On the whole, opinion favoured the setting-up of a full-time course for teachers of the partially sighted in which some instruction on other handicaps would be given. One or two witnesses said that it should be compulsory for teachers of the partially sighted to undertake such a course, as it was already for teachers of the blind.

9.10 Questions about the willingness of teachers in schools and units for the partially sighted to take a course leading to a qualification in teaching the partially sighted were included in a survey which one of our members carried out (see Appendix J). In all 179 assistant teachers and 25 head teachers were included in the survey. Nearly 60% indicated that they would welcome the opportunity to take such a course, and the majority of these stipulated that the course should be part-time. There were 40% who indicated that they would not be prepared to take such a course; about 10% of these considered such a course unnecessary and about 32% made it clear that they did not intend to continue teaching the partially sighted indefinitely.

9.11 A great deal of evidence was received on the subject of short courses for serving teachers of the visually handicapped. These courses are provided by the DES and various other bodies for teachers of the blind and the partially sighted. Some of them serve as ' refresher ' courses for the more experienced teacher and some of them cover special topics. It was found that these courses were widely appreciated and that teachers would like more of them. They would also like to have more opportunities to visit other schools for visually handicapped pupils in order to observe the methods used there. This request was very frequently made and one or two witnesses asked that the need for inter-school visits should be recognised in the number of staff allowed each school. It was also said that teachers, particularly in schools for the partially sighted could benefit from visits to ordinary schools or spells of employment in special schools alternating with spells in ordinary schools. At present the latter proposal involves some difficulty in that teachers receive a supplement to their salary when teaching in special schools.

9.12 Should persons who are themselves visually handicapped be encouraged to train as teachers of visually handicapped children? Very divergent views were put to us on this question.[2] Some people were opposed to any employment of visually handicapped teachers on the grounds that this was a burden to other staff, who had to help the visually handicapped teacher with certain duties which

---

[2] There is a note on blind teachers in schools for the blind in Appendix J., Section 4.

95

only a sighted person can perform, and because in certain circumstances, e.g. fire, it might be unsafe. Most of the witnesses conceded however that there was a place for visually handicapped teachers in schools for the visually handicapped, provided that they did not form too great a proportion of the total staff. It was suggested that a teacher who shares the handicap of his pupils often has special insight into their needs, which is of value not only to himself but also to other teachers with normal sight.

Consideration of the issues

9.13 In their courses of initial training, teachers receive some guidance in dealing with the disabilities that they are likely to meet in ordinary schools. However, we consider that this guidance is not adequate: teachers need to be aware that children may be failing in their studies through visual handicaps and to know of the various services available if further investigation is needed. This instruction should be given in all courses at colleges and departments of education.

9.14 We agree that some experience in ordinary schools is essential before teachers enter schools for the visually handicapped, and we regard a minimum of two years as desirable. It would however be wrong to deter some teachers from entering special education by making a fixed period mandatory; and there is a need for some young teachers in the schools for the visually handicapped. In general, the time at which a teacher will be ready to enter special education will depend upon his age and past experience, including pre-teaching experience. During their later service, teachers should be encouraged to return to ordinary schools for a period, perhaps on a term's secondment.

9.15 The relatively small number of teachers required in schools for the visually handicapped imposes certain constraints on the types of training provided. The supply of teachers needed is a function of three variables: the number of children to be educated, the desired pupil—teacher ratio and the wastage rate among serving teachers. It seems unlikely that there will be much change in the total numbers of blind and partially sighted children to be educated in the foreseeable future (see Chapter 2). We do not propose changes in pupil-teacher ratios: current class sizes (to which some additions have to be made to obtain the appropriate pupil-teacher ratio for a school) on average are about 6 in special schools for the blind and about 9–10 in schools for the partially sighted. Wastage rates are hard to predict, but we received some evidence that staff in schools and further education establishments for the blind stay for fairly long periods. Of a sample of 200 teachers studied in 1969, 32% had taught in their present school for between 6 and 14 years and 23% for 15 years or more. In schools for the partially sighted, of a sample of 204 teachers studied in 1970, 39% had been in their present school for between 6 and 14 years and 15% for 15 years or more (see Appendix J, Section 1).

9.16 In one respect however the facilities for training will require expansion in order to implement our recommendations. We believe that it should be compulsory in future for a teacher who wishes to make a career in teaching the partially sighted to obtain a further qualification, as it is already for a teacher of the blind. Existing teachers of the partially sighted should be encouraged—though not required—to gain the additional qualification. It should bring teachers an extra increment, as does the additional qualification for teachers of the blind. The chief reason why a further course beyond initial teacher training seems to us essential is that teachers require to know more about child development related to partial sight, in order to appreciate the ways in which partially sighted children deviate from the norm and the special problems they face. In addition, teachers need a knowledge of the educational and social implications of different types of visual defects, and a knowledge of the special furniture, equipment and lighting required if partially sighted children are to have the best opportunities to learn.

9.17 We considered whether it should continue to be possible to qualify as a teacher of the blind either by part-time or by full-time training. We agreed that ideally a full-time course should be taken by all teachers, but the arguments already mentioned for the preservation of part-time training are very relevant. They apply to the partially sighted as well (see Appendix J, Section 3, paragraph 4).

9.18 Should any extension be made in the 3-year period in which teachers are at present required to obtain their additional qualification, after taking up a post in a school for the blind? On the whole, we are of the opinion that the 3-year period is about right: it stretches people without putting them under undue strain. There should however be provision for extending the period to 4 years in exceptional circumstances. We also see advantages in splitting the course into two parts. Thus braille, which some teachers put off learning too long, might be examined after the first or second year; and the papers dealing with the application of educational principles to the blind, which tend to be answered thinly if taken too early, could form the second part of the examination.

9.19 How satisfactory are the existing courses? We were able to examine the content and syllabuses of the courses offered by Birmingham University and the College of Teachers of the Blind. The University examination syllabus may need some modification. The course has been evolving since its inception and will no doubt continue to develop, particularly in response to the practical needs of teachers in schools for the visually handicapped. The syllabus of the CTB examination is much too limited, for example, as regards child development; and it seems desirable that the CTB should use a wider range of people as examiners. Teachers taking the CTB course at present cannot be assured adequate tutorial facilities, which often are the responsibility of a hard-pressed head-teacher. A system of visiting tutors might be organised, and also vacation courses. Further the ophthalmic content of both courses may need expansion; and the examining bodies should consult the Faculty of Ophthalmologists about this.

9.20 The incidence of children with multiple handicap in schools for the blind and partially sighted is increasing, as many of our witnesses pointed out. It has been estimated that about half of visually handicapped children have one or more additional handicaps (see paragraph 5.67); and in the Sunshine Home schools the proportion is much greater (see paragraph 4.20). We rely on the courses leading to a further qualification for teaching the visually handicapped to provide at least a general knowledge of the other handicapping conditions likely to be encountered in these schools and of the associated learning and psychological problems. We consider that the course at Birmingham University gives adequate instruction but not the course leading to the CTB Diploma; and teachers of the multi-handicapped with that Diploma need further training such as a one-term course.

9.21 In Chapter 5 the majority of us supported the idea of educating the blind and the partially sighted in the same schools. In such schools it is obviously desirable that some teaching staff should be qualified to teach both groups of children. This points to the need for a common course for teachers of the blind and the partially sighted, and we are glad to see that the Birmingham full-time course has developed on these lines. In the light of the criticisms made of the CTB course, we recommend that the possibility should be studied of replacing the present part-time course by a fuller and better course for teachers of the partially sighted as well as of the blind, run in co-operation with Birmingham University.

9.22 In our view, a variety of training arrangements may be desirable for teachers of the visually handicapped: a full-time course developed from the present Birmingham one; a part-time course based on the University; and a part-time course with some short periods of residence there.

9.23 Considerable anxieties were expressed to us about the career prospects of teachers of the visually handicapped. It was argued that these were to some extent dependent on the type of training which the teacher received. Special schools for the visually handicapped are few in number and mostly small in size. There is a restriction in the number of headships and graded posts available, which seems to apply particularly to women teachers. The teacher seeking promotion may have to look outside the field of the visually handicapped to other kinds of special education or to ordinary schools. It is therefore desirable that training should be as broad as possible, without neglecting its specialist visual handicap content.

9.24 We should like to see teachers in schools for the visually handicapped having more contact with teachers in other types of school. The educational isolation from which many schools suffer was mentioned in paragraph 6.06. Meetings, conferences, teachers' centres and more informal exchange of information and ideas are all valuable. It is desirable as well that refresher courses should be available for teachers who have been in service for a period, and that all such teachers should be encouraged to take them. If the proposals of the James Committee for a 'third cycle' of in-service education and training are implemented, we hope that this will encourage (among other things) the development of a wide variety of courses for teachers of handicapped children.

9.25 Finally, we turned to the question whether people who were themselves visually handicapped should teach children who were. Blind staff should not normally work with partially sighted children, since teachers often have to act as eyes for these children, for example in relation to handwriting, typewriting, lighting, colour work and outside visits. Otherwise, in view of the value which is placed on the work of visually handicapped teachers, we consider that it is undesirable for persons to be barred from teaching posts or training solely on the grounds of visual handicap. All their qualities should be taken into account: trainees need to be of the right personality and to have practical ability and an understanding of children. They should also have teaching experience in sighted schools, in the same way as other teachers of the visually handicapped do. There is however a limitation on the number of blind teachers who can be absorbed in any one school.

RESIDENTIAL CHILD CARE STAFF

The present position
9.26 Since so many visually handicapped children are in boarding schools, considerable responsibility rests upon those adults who look after them out of school hours. Sometimes the adults are teachers but frequently they are child care staff. Whether they are known as housemothers, matrons, assistant matrons, housefathers or residential child care officers, their skill and experience are of the utmost importance in furthering the development of visually handicapped children towards independent living.

9.27 In 1968 there were 244 full-time child care workers in schools for the visually handicapped. Of these 16 were qualified by possessing the Certificate in the Residential Care of Children and Young People awarded by the Central Training Council in Child Care and 15 had been awarded the Certificate of the National Nursery Examination Board. In addition there were State Registered and State Enrolled Nurses but nursing qualifications cannot be assumed to include training in child care. A survey of child care staff in residential special schools in 1970 revealed that only 15% of child care staff in such schools were qualified. At Condover Hall School the Royal National Institute for the Blind has appointed a training officer, holding the Advanced Certificate in the Residential Care of Children and Young People and all housemothers and assistant housemothers at the school are given in-service training appropriate to the need of the pupils.

Consideration of the issues
9.28 It is urgent that child care staff in boarding schools for handicapped children should be qualified, and that their qualification should include appropriate training in helping the boys and girls in the particular group with which the worker is concerned. This specialised training might be part of or might follow the course for a qualification such as the Certificate in the Residential Care of Children and Young People now awarded by the Central Council for Education and Training in Social Work. Since, however, many child care workers in boarding schools for the blind and partially sighted are recruited locally and their initial interest is with visually handicapped children, there is a case for stimulating and maintaining their interest by the provision of in-service training specially concerned with the visually handicapped. Workers trained in this way should later be helped to obtain a recognised qualification in residential child care work, without necessarily first gaining experience in work with normal children.

RECOMMENDATIONS

9.29 We recommend that:

(1) all teachers should be aware that children may be failing in their studies through visual handicap and know where these children should be referred (paragraph 9.13);

(2) teachers (other than existing teachers of the partially sighted) who wish to make a career in teaching the partially sighted should be required to obtain further teaching qualifications through full-time or a part-time course (paragraphs 9.16 and 9.17);

(3) the possibility should be studied of replacing the present part-time training for teachers of the blind by a revised course for teachers of the blind and partially sighted, run in co-operation with Birmingham University (paragraph 9.21);

(4) the training of teachers of the visually handicapped should be as broad as possible (paragraph 9.23);

(5) refresher courses should be available for teachers, who should also be encouraged to take part in local activities at teachers' centres etc. (paragraph 9.24);

(6) persons should not be barred from teaching posts or training solely on the grounds of visual handicap (paragraph 9.25); and

(7) child care staff should have relevant qualifications, and in-service training specially concerned with the visually handicapped should be provided for workers recruited locally (paragraph 9.28).

CHAPTER 10 : RESEARCH

INTRODUCTION

10.01 It is clear from the previous chapters that a considerable body of research work on the problems of the visually handicapped has been carried out and is in operation at this moment. Reference has been made to various enquiries into the characteristics of the visually handicapped and the best methods of educating them; and much of this work has been described and summarized in a report by Mr M. J. Tobin (The Teacher of the Blind, Vol. LIX, Nos. 3 and 4, College of Teachers of the Blind, April and July, 1971).

10.02 We have also received reports on surveys and experimental studies on the following topics: the adequacy of social services for blind children and their parents; tested abilities of blind and partially sighted children; vocabulary and braille reading ability of blind children; effects of oral instruction and programmed learning; sex education of blind children; methods of mobility training; effects of boarding school education; further education and employment of partially sighted school leavers; employment of multiply handicapped blind school leavers; employment of teachers of the blind and partially sighted.

10.03 Although a number of aspects of the problems and education of visually handicapped children has been studied, much further research is required. The investigations which in our view are most urgently called for fall into three categories: I, large-scale surveys; II, psychological studies of the cognitive and emotional characteristics and development of visually handicapped children; III, studies of educational abilities and teaching methods.

I SURVEYS

10.04 It was made clear in Chapter 3 that the procedures for *Identifying, Assessing and Notifying* visually handicapped children were often inadequate and unsatisfactory, and we suggested methods for improving these. It would seem desirable that a detailed continuing survey of these procedures should be initiated, and maintained until they are uniformly satisfactory throughout the country.

10.05 We had great difficulty in obtaining reliable evidence as to the incidence of visually handicapped children with *additional handicaps* other than those in schools and classes for the visually handicapped. It is probable that, since the implementation of the Education (Handicapped Children) Act, 1970, a considerable number of severely mentally handicapped children with visual handicap will come to light. In a survey in 1970–71 in the North Midlands a medical officer of the Department of Education and Science found that, of 2,313 in 38 day schools for these children, 81 (3·5%) were known to have a visual handicap, of which 36 were thought to be blind; also many of these 81 children, in addition to visual and mental handicap, had associated physical and social handicaps. Enquiries are needed to identify all visually handicapped children with other major handicaps, and to discover where and how they are being educated. It may then be possible to devise the most suitable placement for them; but knowledge as to the best methods of educating them, and particularly the severely mentally handicapped, is lacking. Nevertheless, valuable evidence should be accumulating, for instance from the work of Dr Simon at Lea Castle Hospital and Dr C. E. Williams at Borocourt Hospital, and such work should be kept under continued review.

10.06 There appeared to be some disagreement as to whether the prevalence of *emotional maladjustment* was greater among visually handicapped than among sighted children (see paragraph 3.27). Further study of this problem is required; and also of the types of maladjustment occurring in the visually handicapped, the causes of their maladjustment, the methods of dealing with them and (by means of follow-up studies) the efficacy of these methods.

10.07 Because of the lack of relevant information, it is thought desirable that there should be a survey of the numbers of visually handicapped receiving *further education* and what type of further education if any the visually handicapped are receiving.

10.08 Some information is available as to the types of *employment* which visually handicapped children enter on leaving school. Further extensive enquiries however are needed into employment opportunities, especially for the partially sighted.

II PSYCHOLOGICAL STUDIES

10.09 The upbringing and education of visually handicapped children should be related to the peculiar problems created for them by their handicap, and to the best methods of overcoming these and enabling the children to live and work happily after leaving school. But too little is known with certainty as to the nature of these problems.

10.10 It was pointed out at the beginning of Chapter 4 that the conceptual understanding of visually handicapped children, and particularly of children blind from birth or infancy, must inevitably be limited by their restricted knowledge of the nature of the physical environment; of what objects are like and how they are spatially positioned; and of how events are caused. Thus these children's conceptions of reality inevitably differ from those of sighted children; and it is difficult if not impossible for sighted people to realise these differences. But they are likely to produce restrictions also in the capacity of the visually handicapped to respond and adapt to environmental events. Although a number of experiments has been carried out relating to particular problems of adaptation and to special difficulties in learning, no systematic and comprehensive picture has ever been presented as to how blind children conceive of their environment. It should be noted that, although the conceptions of the partially sighted are likely to be less restricted than those of the blind, what they perceive may differ from what is seen by the sighted and these differences require to be investigated.

10.11 It would be of enormous value for understanding the development and planning the education of visually handicapped children that widespread enquiries should be undertaken into all the relevant aspects of these children's understanding and capacity to adapt to the environment. This might include study of problems such as the following :

(i) development of concepts of objects; of space and distance; of shape, number, volume, etc. (e.g. as in Piaget's ' conservation ' experiments); of causes of events.

(ii) verbalization and the realistic use of language; reasoning, concrete and abstract; imagination.

(iii) The relation of these to experiences in early childhood of interaction with parents and activities promoted by parents and parent counsellors; to nursery school activities; to mobility training.

10.12 The capacity of visually handicapped children to react and adapt their behaviour to their particular conceptions is obviously affected by their motivation and their emotions. The following in particular should be studied :

(i) Activation and curiosity in visually handicapped children as compared with those of sighted children; the activities of exploration, discovery, play, manipulation, construction, control and mastery of the environment; avoidance and fear of the unknown; and the effects on all these of different degrees of environmental stimulation and restriction.

(ii) Social adaptation, the arousal and control of aggression and fear, the establishment of normal social relations with adults and children, sighted and visually handicapped; the effects on these of stimulating or restricting social environments.

10.13 It is clear that the establishment of a full understanding of the cognitive, motivational and emotional processes in visually handicapped children, of the differences from sighted children and of the factors which aggravate or minimise these differences, requires very wide and complex investigations, through controlled observations of spontaneous behaviour and experimental procedures. Such a programme of enquiry could be carried out only piecemeal, but a beginning could be made through studies of problems such as those outlined above. Such studies must be performed by experienced psychologists, probably in universities or in special units attached to universities. Enquiries of this kind are in fact in progress in a number of university departments; and it would be most valuable if this work on the visually handicapped could be extended and co-ordinated, and if similar work could be undertaken elsewhere.

III EDUCATIONAL STUDIES

10.14 These fall into two categories. The first consists of studies of the abilities of visually handicapped children to respond to various educational procedures and to undertake various occupations on leaving school :

dies have been made of verbal and non-verbal *intelligence* testing
visually handicapped children and some tests are now available,
ough they may require further standardisation. But tests of *con-
ptual development* would also be valuable; for instance using the
eoretical framework and the methods of investigation of Piaget.

(ii) Existing tests of *verbal ability* for sighted children should be applicable
for the visually handicapped also; but the tendency to use words without
completely realising their concrete meanings needs investigation.

(iii) Some tests of other aptitudes have also been designed, notably Nolan's
roughness discrimination test, which appears to give a useful prediction
of aptitude for learning *braille*. But further investigation of aptitude for
braille would be rewarding. Tests of *mathematical* ability and *mechanical* aptitude (spatial ability or ' k ' factor) would also be valuable.

(iv) For both blind and partially sighted school leavers, investigation should
be made into the type of counselling and methods of *vocational assessment* (including practised tasks for the Blind); and the success of these in
leading to job satisfaction should be ascertained through follow-up
studies. A study of tests for occupational potential should be undertaken by occupational psychologists, such as those working for the
Department of Employment (see paragraphs 8.14 and 8.17). A comprehensive investigation should also be considered to discover whether
a battery of general tests such as those suggested above can produce
adequate predictions of occupational proficiency for both blind and
partially sighted children; or such a battery supplemented by particular
tests predicting efficiency in particular skills and occupations.

10.15 The second category consists of studies of the efficacy of various teaching
methods to which reference has been made in Chapter 7 :

(i) The value of *activity* methods of education for young sighted children
is now generally recognised, and these are employed extensively in the
education of visually handicapped children also. But it would be
valuable to study in detail the particular methods and activities most
appropriate for visually handicapped children of different ages and
degrees of intelligence, and especially to ascertain which activities are
most useful for developing these children's understanding of and
ability to cope with their environment and the demands it makes on
them.

(ii) The teaching of *braille* is obviously one of the most essential and
difficult tasks in the teaching of the blind. Although it has been investigated fairly extensively, there seems to be no general agreement
as to the age, degree of intelligence and of other abilities necessary for
learning braille; whether any one method of teaching is superior to all
others; whether the method be varied according to the children's
abilities; and whether Grade I or Grade II should be employed for
beginners. The best methods of introducing children to the learning
of braille might also be studied. In addition to the question of the
teaching of braille, there should also be further study into the number
and nature of the contractions to be employed in Grade II and into
the development of new methods for the reproduction of braille.

(iii) *Aural learning* methods, especially from tape-recorded material, have also been investigated, and demonstrated to be efficient. But further study would be useful of the types of subject, material and method of presentation most appropriate in aural learning at various ages and for various degrees of intelligence, together with some comparison of the relative effectiveness of braille learning. The value of *programmed learning* for the education of the visually handicapped would also repay investigation.

(iv) Modern methods of teaching *mathematics* and *science* to the blind are described in " The teaching of science and mathematics to the blind,"[1] and one of our members, Mr Marshall, has prepared memoranda on these for the partially sighted. But systematic investigation of the efficacy of these methods for different types of child is required. There is also room for the further study of the design and construction of equipment to be used in scientific practical work for the blind.

(v) A systematic survey of modern methods of teaching *music* is desirable, and an enquiry to discover those which produce the best results for (a) execution, (b) understanding and appreciation and (c) composition. The musically talented require special consideration.

(vi) There are numerous studies of *mobility training*, but further extensive investigation is required to determine which are the best methods and devices for children of different ages and degrees of intelligence. The relation of these to the development of environmental concepts and ability to adapt to the environment should also be investigated fully.

(vii) Numerous *low visual aids* and *audio-visual aids* have been designed for use by the partially sighted and by blind children with residual vision (see Appendices E and G). Their design and use in schools should be systematically investigated.

10.16 The Schools Council might possibly be interested in studying and advising on teaching methods for the visually handicapped, and especially on items iii. and iv. It is recommended that an approach be made to the Schools Council to ascertain whether the Council would be willing to undertake the design of special curricula for both the blind and the partially sighted, including the special needs of the additionally handicapped.

10.17 On many of the problems listed, carefully controlled investigations should be made to determine objectively which are the methods most suitable for teaching various types of visually handicapped children.

10.18 Enquiries of this kind are being carried out at the University of Birmingham Research Centre for the Education of the Visually Handicapped and at the Blind Mobility Research Unit of the University of Nottingham Department of Psychology. It is possible that the enquiries could be extended if these units were expanded. Also, members of certain University Departments and Institutes of Education contribute experimental studies of specific problems.

---

[1] Report to the Viscount Nuffield Auxiliary Fund, obtainable from the Royal National Institute for the Blind.

H

CO-ORDINATION

10.19 We understand that a number of other research projects is being carried out in universities and other establishments. There is need to co-ordinate all research in the field of the education of the visually handicapped, in order to avoid duplication, to ensure that the resources of individual schools are not overtaxed and to secure wide dissemination of the results. Two bodies exist which would carry out some of these functions—the Birmingham University Research Centre for the Education of the Visually Handicapped (mentioned in paragraph 10.18) and the Research Council of the College of Teachers of the Blind. This was set up in 1951 " to initiate, co-ordinate and generally promote research into educational and social problems arising from the handicap of blindness in school children and young persons; and to make known the results of such research from time to time."

RECOMMENDATION

10.20 We recommend that research on the lines suggested in this chapter should be carried out and co-ordination secured of all research into the education of the visually handicapped.

CHAPTER 11 : SUMMARY OF RECOMMENDATIONS

I PLANNING OF EDUCATIONAL SERVICES

11.01 For purposes of planning special school provision for the visually handicapped over the next decade, the total number of places required should be assumed to be approximately the same as at present (paragraph 2.12).

11.02 A national plan should be drawn up for the distribution, organisation and management of special schools and other educational services for the visually handicapped (paragraph 6.10).

11.03 To this end, committees representing the local education authorities should be set up, in regions designated by the Department of Education and Science, to prepare plans on both a short-term and a long-term basis for their region, after consultation with representatives of voluntary bodies and the health services (paragraph 6.10).

11.04 The Department should co-ordinate the regional plans, determine which schools should have a countrywide intake, and establish a national committee to promote and oversee the execution of the national plan (paragraph 6.10).

11.05 The Secretary of State should be empowered, if necessary, by new legislation, to ensure that the recommendations of the national plan are put into effect within a reasonable period of time (paragraph 6.14).

II CHILDREN UNDER 5 AND MEDICAL SERVICES UP TO SCHOOL LEAVING AGE

11.06 All children should be screened for visual handicap at child health clinics as part of a general developmental assessment (paragraph 3.08).

11.07 Children identified as possibly having a visual abnormality should be referred for examination and treatment to the local ophthalmologist who would be a member of a comprehensive district assessment team. Children should receive a paediatric examination from this team, the key members of which should be a paediatrician, an ophthalmologist, a local authority medical officer and, when he could participate, the child's general practitioner, together with an otologist, a health visitor, a social worker, and other experts as required (paragraph 3.08).

11.08 Visually handicapped children should then be referred for combined ophthalmological/educational assessment to a regional assessment team including an ophthalmologist with particular skill and an interest in children, an educational psychologist and a teacher of the visually handicapped (paragraph 3.09).

11.09 Wherever possible, the regional assessment team should examine the visually handicapped child in a school setting (paragraph 3.09).

11.10 Every family of a visually handicapped child under the age of 5 should have access to a team who can meet their different needs for counselling. To this end, local authorities should be responsible for securing an adequate number of staff with the requisite training and experience to provide, for parents of young visually handicapped children in their area, psychological support and advice about the day-to-day handling of their children. These staff should work in close association with the teachers or educational psychologists who would carry out educational counselling and with the regional assessment team, which should co-ordinate their work (paragraphs 4.17 and 4.18).

11.11 All visually handicapped children under 5 should at some stage receive some form of education, and a range of educational facilities should be available in each area, including a peripatetic teaching service (paragraphs 4.33 and 4.34).

11.12 Children under 5 should not board away from home except in very special circumstances; and children in residential units should go home at week-ends whenever possible (paragraphs 4.34 and 4.37).

11.13 All visually handicapped children should be regularly re-assessed (paragraph 3.10).

11.14 Parents should be kept informed about their child's condition and the help he needs (paragraph 3.11).

11.15 A new form of notification of a visual handicap is required and a revised form of certification when a pupil leaves school (paragraph 3.12).

11.16 Vision screening of all children, including annual tests of visual acuity, should be part of school health services in all primary and secondary schools and special schools for other handicaps. The ophthalmic services for visually handicapped children attending these schools must be of the standard provided in a special school for the visually handicapped (paragraph 3.15).

11.17 All schools for the visually handicapped should be visited regularly by a consultant ophthalmologist and an optician working for the National Health Service on a sessional basis, and should be equipped with a suitable examination room. There should be close co-operation between the ophthalmologist and the teaching staff, and between the optician and the ophthalmologist in the supply and maintenance of spectacles and low visual aids (paragraphs 3.18 and 3.19).

11.18 Genetic counselling should be made available to all parents and older visually handicapped children, through either the ophthalmologist in the regional assessment team or the ophthalmologist in each comprehensive assessment team based on a district general hospital (paragraphs 3.24 and 3.25).

11.19 Every school for the visually handicapped should have regular links with a child guidance service or access to a consultant psychiatrist (paragraph 3.29).

11.20 Visually handicapped children should receive a general medical examination more frequently than sighted children; and the school nurse or welfare staff should maintain continuous and close observation of the general health of all children in their care (paragraphs 3.32 and 3.33).

11.21 The local authority school medical and dental services should be made available to all visually handicapped children in day or boarding schools (paragraphs 3.32 and 3.34).

11.22 Local education authorities should receive follow-up medical and educational reports on children sent to schools in other areas; and there should be good communication between the medical services responsible for visually handicapped children at boarding school and in home areas (paragraph 3.35).

III ORGANISATION OF SCHOOLS

11.23 All blind and partially sighted children, except some of those with multiple handicaps or poor home conditions, should live at home if their home is within an hour's journey of a suitable school and provided their parents can be given guidance on child management (paragraph 5.09).

11.24 Where day attendance is impracticable, weekly boarding should be adopted and local education authorities should help with travel home (paragraph 5.10).

11.25 All boarding schools should be prepared to accept children, who normally attend school by day, for boarding for short periods to meet domestic emergencies (paragraph 5.12).

11.26 Further systematic experiments should be carried out, within the context of the national plan, with the education of visually handicapped children in ordinary schools, either in ordinary or in special classes (paragraph 5.31).

11.27 Experiments are desirable, in order to meet regional needs, in the grouping of several schools for children with different handicaps on campus sites, sharing a full range of educational and medical resources, with ordinary schools adjoining (paragraphs 5.36–5.37).

11.28 [1]Blind and partially sighted children would benefit from being educated in the same schools, though they need to be in separate classes at the junior stage (paragraph 5.45).

11.29 Co-education should be adopted for all visually handicapped children throughout their school careers (paragraph 5.50).

11.30 All-age schools are to be preferred where their existence would enable a substantial proportion of children to attend as day pupils instead of boarding away from home, or as weekly boarders instead of going to a boarding school further away where week-end visits home would be impracticable. Otherwise, there should be a mixed pattern of all-age schools and separate primary and secondary schools, varying according to local circumstances (paragraph 5.57).

---

[1] Two members dissent from this recommendation.

11.31 Places should be provided for all visually handicapped children likely to profit from GCE ' O ' and ' A ' level work; courses would be required in only a very few schools, none of which should be as small as the 2 single-sex selective schools for the blind. Other schools should be prepared to cater for children who want to take CSE courses etc. (paragraphs 5.64–5.65).

11.32 A variety of special schools and units should be available for visually handicapped children with additional handicaps. Where such children are accommodated in special schools for the multiply handicapped, due attention and care must be given to their visual handicap (paragraph 5.71).

IV SCHOOL CURRICULUM AND TEACHING AIDS

11.33 Blind children should possess their own Perkins brailler and should retain it when they leave school (paragraph 7.09).

11.34 All visually handicapped children who can benefit from it should be taught to type and they should be provided with their own typewriter when they leave school (paragraphs 7.10 and 7.14).

11.35 Staffing should be sufficiently generous to allow periods of individual teaching for partially sighted children with special difficulties in learning to read (paragraph 7.11).

11.36 Schools for the blind should have braille reproduction equipment. Schools for the partially sighted should have access to an enlarger and to offset litho copying equipment. Technicians should be available for the operation and maintenance of all apparatus and equipment (paragraphs 7.16, 7.18 and 7.30).

11.37 The appropriate Government departments should take urgent steps to ensure that the production of books, including recorded books, for visually handicapped children is fully adequate (paragraphs 7.19 and 7.23).

11.38 Tape recorders and talking books should be available for all visually handicapped children, who should be instructed in their use. If possible, they should have their own cassette tape-recorders on leaving school (paragraphs 7.21 and 7.23).

11.39 Schools for the partially sighted should be equipped with low visual aids for individual children and audio-visual aids. There should be good general lighting and an adjustable system of individual lighting (paragraph 7.12, 7.25, 7.26 and 7.28).

11.40 Local education authorities should make their advisory services available to non-maintained special schools, who should also make use of any other community or advisory resources (paragraph 7.31).

11.41 Consideration should be given to improving the methods of teaching certain subjects, especially the natural sciences (paragraphs 7.32–7.49).

11.42 All visually handicapped children should be encouraged to take part in all forms of physical education which they can enjoy without risk (paragraph 7.51).

11.43 A systematic programme of mobility training should be provided for all partially sighted children who need it, as well as for all blind children (paragraph 7.55).

11.44 All schools for the visually handicapped containing pupils of secondary age should enable as many as possible to take courses for public examinations, including CSE. They should consider adopting CSE Mode III (paragraph 7.60).

V FURTHER EDUCATION, HIGHER EDUCATION AND VOCATIONAL GUIDANCE

11.45 For each visually handicapped child careers guidance should begin at least 2 or 3 years before he leaves school, and for children in residential schools this guidance must be given in close consultation with the careers officers in the pupils' home areas, as well as with parents (paragraphs 8.08 and 8.09).

11.46 For each visually handicapped child there should also be a careers case conference of a team of experts, in liaison with the child's comprehensive assessment team (paragraphs 8.08 and 8.09).

11.47 The assessment team responsible for filling out Form BD8 (or its replacement) when a child leaves school should receive information from the careers officer about his subsequent progress, since this might indicate a need to amend the certificate (paragraph 8.11).

11.48 No blind child should go straight into employment at the age of 16, but there should be additional provision for all to continue full-time education and/or training (whether at school or in some other establishment) until they are at least 17 years old (paragraph 8.12).

11.49 The accommodation, functions and curriculum of the present assessment centres should be reviewed (paragraph 8.13).

11.50 A residential centre should be established, serving the whole country, to provide social training for blind young people who have severe additional handicaps and are not likely to be suited to vocational assessment and training (paragraph 8.15).

11.51 One or more centres should be established for the vocational assessment of the partially sighted, the number and form of which would depend on the results of research (paragraph 8.16).

11.52 Schemes for the part-time attendance at colleges of further education of visually handicapped pupils in their last years at school should be extended (paragraph 8.23).

11.53 Schools for the visually handicapped should maintain close liaison with further and higher education establishments for the sighted to facilitate their assimilation of visually handicapped students (paragraphs 8.23 and 8.24).

11.54 Local education authorities should grant-aid generously, irrespective of help from other sources, visually handicapped students taking courses at universities, colleges of further education and assessment centres (paragraph 8.26).

11.55 More facilities should be provided by local education authorities for informal classes and activities in which visually handicapped adults can participate (paragraph 8.27).

11.56 When the national plan for the education of the visually handicapped is drawn up, the need should be considered for a more even distribution through the regions of the provision required for vocational guidance and assessment, further education and vocational training (paragraph 8.28).

VI TRAINING OF TEACHERS AND RESIDENTIAL CHILD CARE STAFF

11.57 All teachers should be aware that children may be failing in their studies through visual handicap and to know where these children should be referred (paragraph 9.13).

11.58 Teachers (other than existing teachers of the partially sighted) who wish to make a career in teaching the partially sighted should be required to obtain further teaching qualifications through a full-time or a part-time course (paragraphs 9.16 and 9.17).

11.59 The possibility should be studied of replacing the present part-time training for teachers of the blind by a revised course for teachers of the blind and partially sighted, run in co-operation with Birmingham University (paragraph 9.21).

11.60 The training of teachers of the visually handicapped should be as broad as possible (paragraph 9.23).

11.61 Refresher courses should be available for teachers who should also be encouraged to take part in local activities at teachers' centres etc. (paragraph 9.24).

11.62 Persons should not be barred from teaching posts or training solely on the grounds of visual handicap (paragraph 9.25).

11.63 Child care staff should have relevant qualifications, and in-service training specially concerned with the visually handicapped should be provided for workers recruited locally (paragraph 9.28).

VII RESEARCH

11.64 Research on the lines suggested in Chapter 10 should be carried out and co-ordination secured of all research into the education of the visually handicapped (paragraph 10.20).

LIST OF WITNESSES

The symbol † opposite certain individuals denotes that both oral and written evidence was given. All other organisations and other individual witnesses sub-mitted written evidence only, apart from two individuals (as indicated) who gave oral evidence only.

(i) ORGANISATIONS

Association of Blind and Partially Sighted Teachers and Students

Association of Chief Education Officers

Association of Education Committees

Association for Education of the Visually Handicapped (USA)

Association of Municipal Corporations

Association for Special Education

Birmingham Royal Institution for the Blind

Board of Management and Staff, Derby School for Partially Sighted Children, Preston

British Medical Association

British Paediatric Association

British Psychological Society

Civil Service Commission Research Unit, Civil Service Department

Conference of Head Teachers of the Blind

Consultative Committee of the Head Teachers of ILEA Schools for the Partially Sighted

Corporation of Edinburgh Education Authority

Corporation of Glasgow Education Authority

Council for the Training of Health Visitors

Council for Training in Social Work

County Councils Association

Department of Employment

Department of Health and Social Security

Department of National Health and Welfare, Canada

Educational Institute of Scotland

Faculty of Ophthalmologists of the Royal College of Surgeons, England

General Executive, College of Teachers of the Blind

Governors, Chorleywood College

Governors, Royal Normal College for the Blind

Governors, Royal School for the Blind, Liverpool

Governors and Staff, West of England School for the Partially Sighted, Exeter

Governors, Worcester College for the Blind

Hampstead Child-Therapy Clinic

Head Teachers' Conference, Schools for the Blind, United Kingdom and Eire

Hunter College, New York

Initial Teaching Alphabet Foundation

Inner London Education Authority

Library Association

Management Services (Training) Division, Civil Service Department

National Association for the Education of the Visually Handicapped

National Association for the Education of the Partially Sighted

National Association of Head Teachers

National Association of Social Welfare Officers of the Blind of England and
Wales

National Children's Home

National Federation of the Blind of the United Kingdom

National Mobility Centre

National Society for Mentally Handicapped Children

National Union of Teachers

Nippon Lighthouse Welfare Centre for the Blind, Osaka, Japan

Paediatric Department, United Oxford Hospitals

Parent Teacher Association, Joseph Clarke School for the Partially Sighted

Research Committee of the College of Teachers of the Blind

Royal London Society for the Blind

Royal National Institute for the Blind

School Broadcasting Council for the United Kingdom

Schools Music Association

School Teachers' Examinations Board of the College of Teachers of the Blind

Society of Medical Officers of Health

Society of Teachers of the Deaf

Spastics Society

Special Education Panel of the Kent County Association of Teachers (NUT)

Training Council for Teachers of the Mentally Handicapped

Wilberforce Home for Multiple-handicapped Blind

(ii) SCHOOLS AND UNITS FOR THE VISUALLY HANDICAPPED IN ENGLAND AND WALES

Evidence was received from all the schools listed in sections i, ii and iii of
Appendix B and also from the following:

(a) Schools for the partially sighted

Barclay School for Partially Sighted Girls, Berkshire — now closed

Whitney School, London — now closed

114

(b) **Special schools with partially sighted children in attendance**
Black-a-Moor Special School, Blackburn
Claremont Open-Air School, Salford
Newman Open-Air School, Rotherham
Northfield Open-Air School, York
South Bristol Open-Air School, Bristol

(c) **Partially sighted unit attached to ordinary school**
Central High School, Manchester — unit now closed

(iii) INDIVIDUALS

Dr M. L. J. Abercrombie
S. E. Armstrong
A. Aston
L. C. Barham
Rev. B. G. Bartlett
J. L. Bashton
G. E. Berry
B. D. A. Best
Miss I. Bird
D. Blasch
D. Blunkett
Dr Werner Boldt
Mrs. P. M. Burgess
Dr D. Campbell
Y. Cassignac
†Miss E. K. Chapman
†Miss E. J. Clarke
P. W. F. Coleman
Miss M. Connelly
Miss L. R. Cox
R. Craig
†W. Cunliffe
†Miss W. E. Deavin
P. Edwards
Dr Dorothy Egan
J. P. Eskdale
B. Ferris
Mrs M. S. Fisher
K. S. Fleet
†Dr R. M. Forrester
Mr and Mrs G. Fosterjohn
Dr Merle Frampton
A. I. Friedmann
R. Fukumoto
†P. A. Gardiner
†Miss N. Gibbs
T. Gissler

Miss I. D. R. Gregory
H. Hayes
B. Hewitt
*Miss A. A. Hill
Miss M. S. Hopper
*Dr C. B. Huss
K. N. K. Jussawala
P. B. Johnstone
Miss E. M. Jones
Dr M. L. Kellmer Pringle
Dr W. J. Kooyman
Dr I. W. Langan
Dr J. N. Langdon
R. G. Lansdown
Dr J. A. Leonard
Dr J. D. Longmore
Dr M. E. MacGregor
Dr R. C. MacKeith
Miss D. McHugh
G. J. I. Miller
M. Milligan
Miss S. Mitchell
B. Mokleby
A. Monrad-Frantzen
Miss J. E. Morris
Mrs K. Murkin
†S. O. Myers
H. R. Nayler
Miss S. Osborne
E. W. Page
Sir James Pitman
J. H. Rigby
Professor R. Roaf
Mrs M. Roper
J. Rundle
G. E. Salisbury
Professor C. Satoh
T. L. Seed
Dr S. Sereni
Mrs A. Sergeant
†Dr Mary D. Sheridan
Miss J. Shields
†Dr G. B. Simon
D. C. Slater
J. Smethurst
Mrs V. Smethurst
Professor Arnold Sorsby
Miss J. Stonehouse
Mrs B. Taylor

---

* Gave oral evidence only.

T. J. C. Taylor
Mrs M. Tew
M. J. Tobin
F. H. G. Tooze
R. G. Turner
V. H. Vaughan
Miss L. Ward
P. Wells
B. J. Wilkinson
Miss J. Wilkinson
†Dr C. E. Williams
T. Williams
C. Wilson
N. H. Winterbottom
Dr Grace E. Woods
Miss J. Wragg
Professor O. L. Zangwill

LIST OF SPECIAL SCHOOLS AND CLASSES AND FURTHER EDU-
CATION ESTABLISHMENTS FOR THE VISUALLY HANDICAPPED
IN ENGLAND AND WALES

The symbol † indicates that the school or establishment has been visited by the
Chairman and/or members of the Committee.

(i) SCHOOLS FOR THE BLIND

Maintained

†Linden Lodge School, London
†Tapton Mount School, Sheffield

Non-maintained

Beechcroft Towse Sunshine House Nursery School, East Grinstead
†Benwell Royal Victoria School, Newcastle-upon-Tyne
†Chorleywood College, Rickmansworth
†Condover Hall School, Shrewsbury
†Dorton House School, Seal, near Sevenoaks
Henshaw's School, Harrogate
†Lickey Grange School, Bromsgrove
†Overley Hall Sunshine House Nursery School, Wellington
†Royal Normal College, Albrighton Hall, near Shrewsbury
†Royal School, Wavertree, Liverpool
Rushton Hall School, Kettering
Sunshine House Nursery School, Southport
†Sunshine House Nursery School, Leamington Spa
†Sunshine House Nursery School, Northwood
Tenovus Sunshine House Nursery School, Bridgend
†Worcester College, Worcester

(ii) SCHOOLS FOR THE BLIND AND PARTIALLY SIGHTED

†School for Visually Handicapped Children, Bridgend (Maintained)
†St. Vincent's School, Liverpool (Non-maintained)

(iii) SCHOOLS FOR THE PARTIALLY SIGHTED

Maintained

Barbara Priestman School, Sunderland
†Clapham Park School, London
†East Anglian School, Gorleston-on-Sea
†Exhall Grange School, Coventry
†George Auden School, Birmingham
†Holmrook School, Liverpool
†John Aird School, London
Joseph Clarke School, London
†Nansen School, London

†New River School, London
†Priestley Smith School, Birmingham
Shawgrove School, Manchester
South Lodge School, Leicester
St. Luke's School, Croydon
Temple Bank School, Bradford
Wold Road School, Kingston-upon-Hull

Non-maintained

Blatchington Court, Seaford
Derby School, Preston
†West of England School, Exeter

(iv) SCHOOLS FOR THE DELICATE AND PHYSICALLY HANDI-CAPPED ADMITTING PARTIALLY SIGHTED PUPILS (ALL MAINTAINED)

Black-a-Moor Special School, Blackburn
Claremont Open-Air School, Salford
†Cleadon Park School, South Shields
Katherine Elliot School, Shrewsbury
Newman Open-Air School, Rotherham
Northfield Open-Air School, York
Park Dean School, Oldham
†Pendower Hall School, Newcastle-upon-Tyne
South Bristol Open-Air School, Bristol

(v) MAINTAINED ORDINARY SCHOOLS CONTAINING SPECIAL CLASSES FOR THE PARTIALLY SIGHTED

Beckett Park Junior Mixed School, Leeds
†Brook Comprehensive School, Sheffield
†Frederick Bird Secondary Modern School, Coventry
Llanedeyrn Primary School, Cardiff
†Moseley Infants' School, Coventry
†Moseley Junior School, Coventry
St Helen's School, Swansea
†Stradbroke Primary School, Sheffield

(vi) ESTABLISHMENTS FOR FURTHER EDUCATION AND TRAIN-ING (ALL NON-MAINTAINED)

†Hethersett Centre, Reigate
†Queen Alexandra College, Harborne, Birmingham
†Royal Normal College, Rowton Castle, near Shrewsbury

119

APPENDIX C

STATISTICS

Figure 1

AGE OF PUPILS IN SPECIAL SCHOOLS (BLIND) AS AT 1 JAN 1971
(Source: DES)

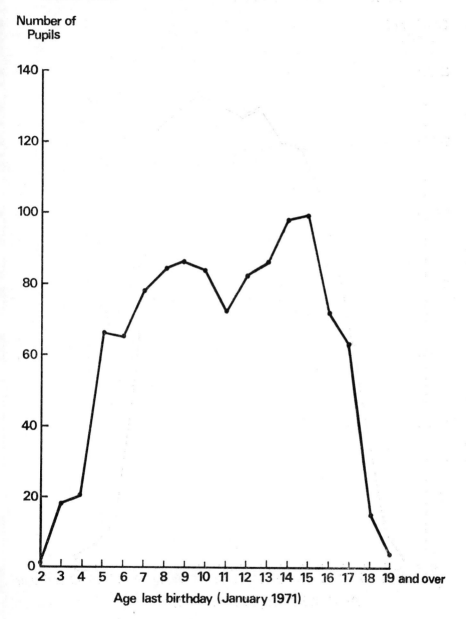

Number of
  Pupils

Age last birthday (January 1971)

121

I

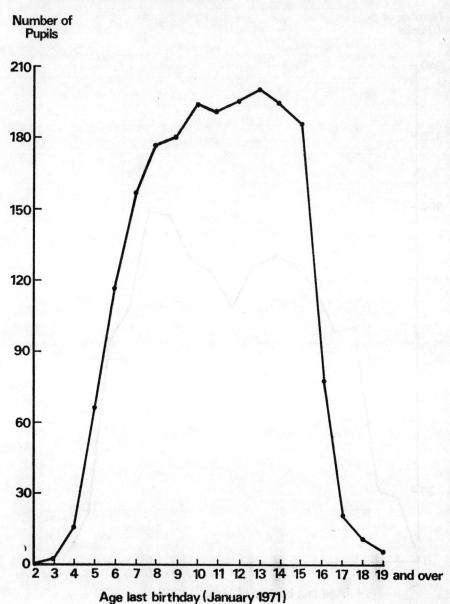

Figure 2

AGE OF PUPILS IN SPECIAL SCHOOLS(PARTIALLY SIGHTED)
AS AT 1 JAN 1971 (Source: DES)

Number of
Pupils

Age last birthday (January 1971)

Figure 3

COMPARATIVE REGIONAL DISTRIBUTION OF VISUALLY
HANDICAPPED CHILDREN AND SPECIAL SCHOOL
PLACES (JANUARY 1970)

(Source: DES)

BLIND

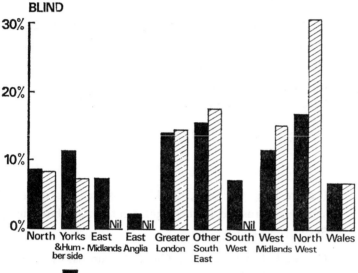

■ %Distribution of children receiving or requiring special education

▨ %Distribution of places in schools for the blind or partially sighted (excluding
schools for the blind with a national intake, i.e. the Sunshine Home Schools, Rushton
Hall, Condover Hall, Chorleywood, Worcester and the Royal Normal College).

PARTIALLY SIGHTED

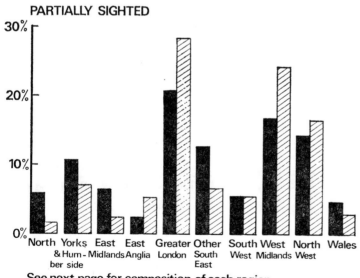

See next page for composition of each region

123

North :	Cumberland, Durham, Northumberland, Westmorland, Yorkshire (North Riding).
Yorkshire and Humberside :	Yorkshire (East and West Ridings), City of York, Lincolnshire (Lindsey).
East Midlands :	Derbyshire, Leicestershire, Lincolnshire (Holland, Kesteven and Lincoln CB), Northamptonshire, Nottinghamshire, Rutland.
East Anglia :	Cambridgeshire and Isle of Ely, Huntingdon and Peterborough, Norfolk, Suffolk (East and West).
Greater London :	Greater London Council area.

Other

South East :	Bedfordshire, Berkshire, Buckinghamshire, Essex, Hampshire, Hertfordshire, Isle of Wight, Kent, Oxfordshire, Surrey, Sussex (East and West).
South West :	Cornwall, Devon, Dorset, Gloucestershire, Isles of Scilly, Somerset, Wiltshire.
West Midlands :	Herefordshire, Shropshire, Staffordshire, Warwickshire, Worcestershire.
North West :	Cheshire, Lancashire.
Wales :	includes Monmouthshire.

Figure 4

NUMBERS OF VISUALLY HANDICAPPED CHILDREN RECEIVING AND
REQUIRING SPECIAL EDUCATION 1961–1980(Source DES)

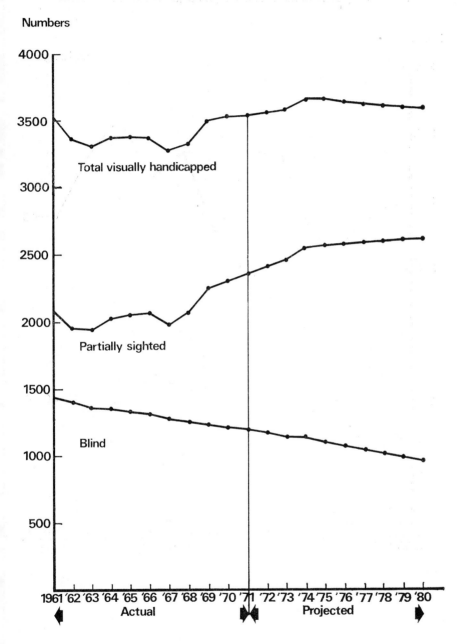

Figure 5

NEW REGISTRATIONS BY AGE 1959-1970 (Partially sighted)

(Source: Registers of the Partially Sighted 1959-1970)

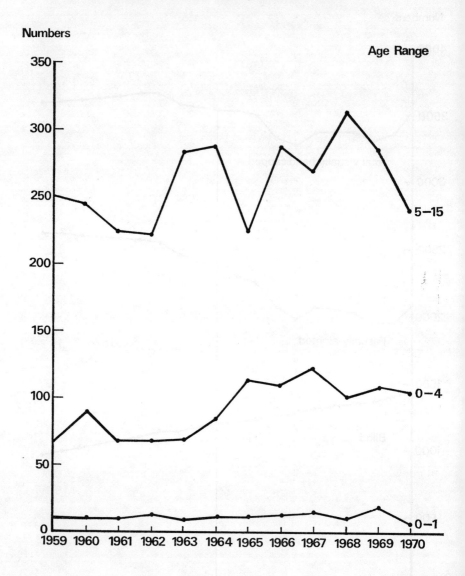

Figure 6
NEW REGISTRATIONS BY AGE 1955-1970 (BLIND)
(Source: REGISTERS OF THE BLIND 1955-1970)

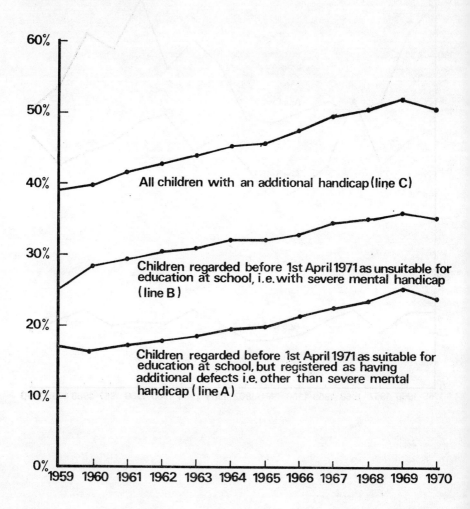

Figure 7
PREVALENCE OF OTHER DEFECTS AMONG BLIND CHILDREN AGED 5-15
(Source: REGISTERS OF THE BLIND 1959-1970)

%age of total registered
population of blind children
between ages of 5-15

All children with an additional handicap (line C)

Children regarded before 1st April 1971 as unsuitable for education at school, i.e. with severe mental handicap (line B)

Children regarded before 1st April 1971 as suitable for education at school, but registered as having additional defects i.e. other than severe mental handicap (line A)

FIGURE 8

PREVALENCE OF OTHER HANDICAPS AMONG PARTIALLY SIGHTED CHILDREN

All schools for the partially sighted and classes or units attached to ordinary or other special schools were asked in 1969 to complete a questionnaire on the numbers of their children with additional handicaps.

Of a total of 1,916 children, 449 had a second handicap sufficient in itself to warrant special educational treatment, i.e. over 23% of all partially sighted children. The following is a breakdown into broad categories of these children:

Handicap								*Numbers*
ESN ..	..	..	..	..	..	..	..	155
Physical handicap	..	..	..	..	..	..		47
Speech defect ..	..	..	..	..	..	..		31
Epilepsy	..	..	..	..	..	..		25
Maladjusted		..	..	..	..	..		25
Hearing defect		..	..	..	..	..		18
Delicate	..	..	..	..	..	..		9
Speech defect and low IQ	..		..	..	..	..		56
Speech defect and hearing defect		..		..	..	..		53
Physical handicap and low IQ			..	..	..	..		30
								449

A further 423 children had other defects which, although on their own they did not call for special educational treatment, created educational problems in conjunction with partial sight.

MODIFICATION OF FORM BD8

1 The Form BD8 may require the ophthalmologist to commit himself too heavily on some aspects of the clinical problem presented by a visually handicapped child on the one hand, but provide insufficient information regarding his visual potential on the other. The former problem may be severe enough to prevent the form being completed as soon as desirable, particularly when the diagnosis is obscure or the assessment of visual acuity difficult. Memories of past mistakes on the part of the doctor, often combined with parental reluctance to accept a tragic situation, may also contribute to delay. One may conclude that this is a formidable problem from study of the ages of first registration of children as blind or partially sighted. There is a significant rise in the numbers of new blind registration at the age of five, when starting at school makes the problem unavoidable, but new registrations of partially sighted children do not show such a proportional increase. For the partially sighted the registration bulge continues in considerable numbers for several years after the age of five, until the child has unhappily demonstrated that he does not have the visual capacity to compete with his sighted contemporaries. He is then transferred, anything up to two years in arrears academically, to a school for the partially sighted. When the present Form BD8 has been completed, the defects in the information on visual acuity provide another potential source of delay before the education authorities can decide on the correct placement of the child. Visual attainment may have to be assessed by trial and error in the classroom, sometimes over a lengthy period that could have been reduced by more comprehensive information at the outset.

2 The Form BD8 derives its visual standard from the Snellen chart. The assessment of the visual acuity of the vast majority of children under the age of five, however, can only be in terms of Snellen equivalents. Section A3 requesting estimates of vision for right and left eyes, unaided, with correcting glasses, and " with both eyes together (the best vision after correction) ", asks for more detail than is necessary for identification of a visual handicap, or which it may be possible to obtain.

3 The present BD8 asks for no information on near vision. Partially sighted education depends on near vision to a major degree, and the acuity of a child's near vision is not to be judged by the defects in his distance (Snellen) vision.

4 The BD8 requests information on the state of the visual field but does not differentiate between right and left hemianopia or altitudinal defects*. Visual field estimation may be difficult in children but simple confrontation will show major defects. A child with a left homonymous hemianopia* will learn to read quite easily because he can scan ahead of the word he is reading with the re-

---

* Hemianopia is a condition in which half the visual field of one eye is missing or blind, most commonly the right or left half. If both eyes are similarly affected, e.g. with right hemianopia, this would be referred to as a right homonymous hemianopia. Hemianopia may also less commonly be altitudinal, in which case either the upper or lower half of the visual field would be blind. For example, an inferior altitudinal hemianopia is a defect in which the patient cannot see anything below his fixation point.

maining right half of his visual field. A child with a right-sided hemianopia cannot do this and has great difficulty in learning to read. The side of the visual field defect can thus make the difference between educating a child as blind or partially sighted, or between totally blind education and blind education using residual vision. Altitudinal defects are just as important. A child with an inferior altitudinal defect, who cannot see anything below the horizontal will be severely handicapped, because the lower half of the visual field is of much greater practical value than the upper half. A child with a superior altitudinal defect may pass for normal by comparison.

5 Insufficient attention is drawn to the presence of other physical or neurological defects that may co-exist with the visual handicap. These may easily prevent full exploitation of residual vision, for example by poor head control or uncontrolled ocular movements, or deficiencies in visuo-spatial co-ordination or absence of limbs.

6 As mentioned in Chapter 3 we feel that the purposes of identification of a visually handicapped child a new form for " Notification of Visual Handicap (NVH) " should be devised. The NVH form should request information as follows :

(a) personal details;

(b) means of referral to the ophthalmologist;

(c) history of the visual defect;

(d) estimation of the visual acuity, for distance in Snellen or Snellen equivalents, for near vision if possible in Times Roman or equivalents;

(e) estimation of the visual field, with details of vertical or lateral defects; and

(f) definitive or presumptive diagnosis.

7 The Form BD8 would be filled in at the age of 16; and it would therefore be possible to retain it largely in its present form with the following alterations:

(i) deletion of the recommendations regarding education; and

(ii) provision of sections requesting information on near vision and additional information on visual field defects, since both these parameters have considerable application to employability as well as to education.

LOW VISUAL AIDS

Types of low visual aid currently available

1 Although there are many variants and refinements in individual low visual aids (LVAs), there are in practice two main types in current use: those which are hand-held or hand-manipulated, and those which are worn on a spectacle frame.

2 Hand magnifiers may be portable, or mounted on a stand. When stand-mounted the reading material is either slid underneath the magnifier or the instrument is pushed across the page. Many of these are quite bulky and some are self-illuminated. They are particularly useful when hand control is imperfect or the depth of focus of the lens is restricted. Hand-held magnifiers are used for both near and distance vision. For near vision they depend on good hand control; most of these are light and easily portable. For distance vision small telescopes are available that allow such objects as numbers on buses to be identified quickly and easily, without encumbering the user with a bulky appliance.

3 Spectacle-mounted LVAs may consist of simple magnifying lenses but more commonly consist of compound lens systems. Of necessity these latter are more bulky, more conspicuous and heavier than conventional spectacles. They are capable of considerably more magnification than hand magnifiers. They may be either uniocular or binocular, and bifocal, trifocal, or separate near and distance vision variants exist. Some of the higher-powered systems are self-illuminated. In most types it is possible to incorporate the patients' own optical correction in the lens system. In recent years efforts have been made to reduce their weight by using plastic lenses instead of glass, and to design frames and lens systems that were less bulky and thus less conspicuous. Improvements in lens design have also reduced the optical aberrations present in earlier versions. Contact lenses may also be used in conjunction with special spectacles. The contact lens forms the posterior part of a Galilean telescope and the spectacle lens the anterior. This system however is complex and for reasons explained below has limited application.

Care and maintenance of low visual aids

4 The optical qualities of the eye may change rapidly, often during periods of rapid growth, and a constant assessment of the refractive state of the patient is essential. Otherwise the value of an LVA may diminish rapidly even though the appliance itself is well maintained. We feel it is the ultimate responsibility of the ophthalmologist to see that continual visual reassessment is maintained throughout school life.

5 Even LVAs that are correctly prescribed can become ineffective in a short time. Rough handling may alter the alignment of the lenses, with disastrous optical effects, particularly if an astigmatic correction is incorporated. The lenses may become scratched or loose in their frame. Loose or ill-fitting side pieces can result in the lenses sagging down the nose, with consequent discomfort and considerable increase in the back vertex distance (BVD), i.e. the distance be-

tween the front of the eye and the back of the spectacle lens. Lenses are pre-scribed to a BVD that is specific for each individual, and alteration (usually an increase) in this has grave effects upon the optical effectiveness of the appli-ance. For example, a long-sighted (hypermetropic) spectacle correction be-comes more powerful the further it is separated from the eye. On the other hand, side pieces that are too tight round the ears, or which cause pressure on the temples or nose, are uncomfortable and will lead to the LVA being discarded. Contact lenses also need careful supervision to ensure accurate fitting. Patients who are wearing contact lenses as part of a Galilean system require particular care to ensure that the back vertex distance remains constant, and that the positioning of their spectacle lenses is accurate so that the optical centres are exactly opposite the patient's eyes.

6 Although the ultimate responsibility for the pupils' visual aid lies with the ophthalmologist, we feel that the most suitable person to supervise this routine maintenance is an optician with special experience in low visual aids and con-tact lenses. It may be difficult to find opticians with both these special interests, in which case two people will be required to work in close collaboration. As however the prescribing of the aid is the responsibility of the ophthalmologist, it is not essential that the optician should be an ophthalmic (i.e. sight-seeing) optician as well as a dispensing optician (i.e. one who only dispenses glasses to a prescription given to him). The optician should be readily available, and in any case should visit the school weekly. It is essential that there should be close collaboration between him and the ophthalmologist.

The value and application of low visual aids

7 Theoretically, many partially sighted or blind children with residual vision should be able to read or see distant objects with an LVA when otherwise they would be unable to do so. In practice, only a proportion achieve this goal. Low intelligence, lack of self-confidence or persistence and even vanity, shyness or a psychological inhibition may prevent them from achieving their potential.

8 Many children start to use an LVA and then discard it after a variable period. There are a variety of reasons for this :

(a) The visual reward may not justify the effort involved in using the ap-pliance;

(b) the LVA may become damaged and thus less effective, and the child lose the habit of using it and be unable to face the effort of reacclimati-sation when it is mended—this is particularly likely to happen if he has passable visual attainments without an LVA, irrespective of the fact that he is not achieving his full visual potential;

(c) his optical condition may change, thus reducing the effectiveness of the appliance;

(d) social pressures from other children may lead him to regard his LVA as unbecoming or unmanly.

9 The pressures mentioned in paragraph 8(d) operate particularly at puberty. Many children use their LVAs with good effect until this age, after which they become more self-conscious, and occasional use of their appliance in public is

restricted to the more intelligent. When outside the school boundary the commonest LVAs in use are the small telescope that can be concealed in the hand or pocket, and the small magnifying glass. Even in the classroom, a spectacle magnifier that has been in constant use up to puberty may only be worn when absolutely necessary, although in the privacy of the bedroom it may be worn continually for close work.

10 Quite distinct from the more human aspects of wearing LVAs are the more technical problems of comfort and visual reward :

   (i) Comfort is still a problem. The larger telescopic spectacles are still too heavy to wear for more than half an hour with comfort, but great improvements have come with the more widespread use of plastics, both for the lenses and their surrounding structures. Nevertheless it is still a strain to wear most of the aids currently available for long periods. Not only is pressure on the bridge of the nose distressing, but bad fitting round the ears rapidly may cause discomfort, and if the child eases the spectacle away from his ears down his nose, it either drops off or becomes optically ineffective because of the increase in the back vertex distance. Quite distinct from their weight and comfort, the sheer bulk of some aids makes them cumbersome and inconvenient to carry. Here also considerable progress has been made; reduction in weight has often been accompanied by a similar reduction in size.

   (ii) Optical magnification presents problems to the wearers of any LVA. The higher the magnification, the more restricted the visual field; the shorter the working distance, the more shallow the depth of focus, the greater the problem of illumination and the more irritating the optical imperfections due to lens distortions in the periphery of the visual field. Figures derived from interrelating these parameters are significant. The vast majority of LVAs supplied give a magnification ranging from 1·0X to 4·5X, the most frequently dispensed being 2·0X to 3·0X. With these latter magnifications the working distances vary widely according to the appliance, ranging from 18cm. to 8cm. approximately, with a depth of focus between 5mm. to 7mm. and a visual field of between 8cm. to 12cm. in diameter. Peripheral lens distortion is negligible and illumination little problem. With a rise in magnification to 8X however conditions are more difficult. The working distance ranges from 2·8cm. to 8cm. according to the type of LVA, the visual field range varies from 2·5cm. to 3·5cm. and the depth of focus may be barely a millimetre. In other words, the child whose appliance has a depth of focus of one millimetre can only move the paper he is reading either half a millimetre towards or away from him before it starts to go out of focus. In the higher ranges of aid currently available, for example 20X, the working distance may be little more than a centimetre, the field of vision only slightly larger and the depth of focus as low as a tenth of a millimetre. While magnification alone brings problems of illumination, the reduction in working distance aggravates the situation enormously. As a result high magnification aids often require built-in illumination. Just as serious is the drastic reduction in depth of focus that accompanies the increase in image size. As will be realised from earlier remarks, it is quite unrealistic to expect a child to maintain a working distance of, for example, three centimetres and to maintain this, holding the book by hand with the depth of focus of one millimetre, providing a margin of error of half a millimetre either way before the object under view goes out of focus. Help must be provided. The commonest way is to design the LVA so that when the reading material is in contact with its anterior surface it is in focus. This adds further to the bulk and weight of the appliance.

While the above comments relate to the optical problems of LVAs applied to near vision, or more specifically reading, the optical problems concerned with distance vision are in many respects similar. Telescopic spectacles have their working distance set at infinity, but their restricted visual field makes them dangerously impractical for constant everyday wear. They may be of value when the wearer is stationary (perhaps watching a television programme) when he may also be able to support their weight with his hands, as when sitting at a table or perhaps at a football match or on a similar occasion; but in general the use of these spectacles is limited.

Conclusion

11 Current difficulties have been frankly explained; and we recognise that the rate of increase in the use of low visual aids will be greatly influenced by the extent to which technical obstacles can be eliminated. Much progress however has been made in recent years, notably in :

(a) the manufacture of lenses that reduce or eliminate optical distortions and aberrations in the periphery of the lens, thus increasing the effective diameter of the visual field of the appliance;

(b) the recognition of the importance of accurate dispensing of LVAs to ensure accurate fitting of the appliance opposite the patient's eyes and at the appropriate distance from the eyes (i.e. the back vertex distance);

(c) the introduction of plastic into the manufacture of both the lenses and the body of the aid, thus reducing weight and increasing wearing time and comfort; and

(d) improvements in the cosmetics of many aids so that they look more like normal spectacles.

We hope that this progress will continue.

SURVEY OF BRAILLE READING

1 The purpose of the survey, which was begun in October, 1969 and completed in July, 1970, was to gather information on the rates of braille readers at secondary school level. The test selected for this purpose was Ballard's Silent Reading Test together with the Completion Test. The only modifications made were those dictated by the use of braille and those for individual rather than group administration. The test consists of a continuous story graded in difficulty. The subject is given an allotted time for reading (4 minutes for braille readers), the story is then removed and replaced by a copy with a number of blanks which have to be suitably filled. Rate of reading in words per minute and a score for comprehension can thus be obtained.

2 Field work took in all schools and colleges in England and Wales for the visually handicapped who use braille as a medium of education. All pupils within an age-range 10 to 18 years at the time of testing were interviewed, giving a total of 625 subjects. By kind permission of the Head Teacher of Redwell County Secondary School, South Shields, two groups of sighted children, 11-year and 14-year-olds (57 subjects in all), were also included.

3 Of the 488 visually-handicapped subjects in the age-range 10–16 years who were interviewed, 40% were unable to cope with the test. In a substantial number of these cases there was mental handicap present in addition to the visual defect, and this would no doubt contribute to low attainment in reading. Other obviously contributory factors such as late entry to, and frequent absences from, school were encountered, as well as factors pertaining to specific situations. Examples were : switches from one medium to another; both print and braille used concurrently and little facility gained with either; lack of conviction of the suitability of braille for individual children and; lack of policy with regard to braille reading, particularly apparent in the break between primary and secondary school.

4 In comparison with the visually-handicapped group of 11-year-olds, approximately 36% of whom had not yet mastered the mechanics of reading sufficiently well to attempt the test, the group of sighted 11-year-olds were all able to read, at least, the first few lines of the story.

5 The above findings indicate the urgent need for remedial teaching in braille reading.

6 About 60% of the eleven-year-olds able to read braille gained a rate of 70 words or over per minute and thereafter there was steady progress until at 16 years of age the percentage was 88, with an increased proportion reading 100 words and over per minute. Data from age-groups 17 and 18 years confirm that, with narrative requiring to be carefully read, a rate of 100 words per minute can be considered as fairly normal.

7 Data from comparative age-groups of sighted and visually handicapped children showed that, while differences in mean comprehension scores were

slight and not statistically significant, mean reading rates differed very significantly, those of the sighted being slightly more than twice those of the visually handicapped.

8 These results indicate that in public examinations time allowance for reading, in relation to the braille content of the paper, should be given to visually-handicapped students.

K

AUDIO-VISUAL AIDS

1 The value of audio-visual aids with normally seeing children is unquestioned. The value of many such aids for the partially sighted is enormous but, as in all else in dealing with partially sighted children, they must be selected with care and tested carefully, bearing in mind the individual visual problems. Audio-visual aids are in no way a substitute for a teacher, rather they demand from the teacher much preparation, evaluation and follow-up. It is the intention here to set out briefly a selection of the various types of such aids, mentioning successful application of them to partially sighted children. This is not to say, however, that these are the only such aids of value to partially sighted children, or that the uses outlined are the only ones. By experiment and adaptation, teachers will be able to extend and enhance their value.

2 There are firstly, the obvious audio-visual aids, such as *Radio and TV broadcasts*. Chosen with care and monitored by the teacher, they can be of great value. A large screen TV is essential if more than a handful of partially sighted children are to receive any benefit. Some firms, too, produce such TVs with their own built-in trolley. TV screens may be built into classroom walls. Care should be taken in moving TV sets on trolleys: they are often liable to topple when being moved over uneven surfaces. One problem of both radio and TV is in having to adapt the timetable to fit in with broadcast times. To obviate this, tape-recordings (both sound and vision) can be made. The tapes can then be drawn upon as and when required. The great advantage of this system is that the broadcast can be used more than once, for deeper study or as a refresher. Of equal value, but unfortunately of very much greater price, is the video tape-recorder which can be used to tape TV broadcasts. Combined with large screen monitors, these are of enormous value. Four children can share a monitor, and so thoroughly appreciate a TV broadcast, whether live or taped.

3 Of course, *tape recorders* (including cassette tape recorders) have a much wider application for partially sighted pupils than just to record broadcasts. Staff can record poetry, books, etc. and pupils can record from play-readings, etc. Talks and criticisms can be recorded, not only by staff and pupils but by outside experts. Local repertory companies and dramatic societies are usually more than willing to help with recordings too. By these methods a sound tape library can be built up, rather like a reference library. A relatively cheap development which is of value with partially sighted pupils is a small unit whereby any number of children up to six can plug in to a tape recorder, and by means of a cheap, plastic, but most reliable, stethoscope, can listen in silence, without any disturbance to the remainder of a class or group. This is a great help with small group, and individual, study, especially of the remedial type. It can be used extensively for private study purposes, too.

4 The *induction loop system* is a further development of the use of a tape recorder. Besides a tape recorder, a special headset with built-in induction receiver, for each pupil, and a loop or wire are required. The loop may be fixed to the ceiling, or may be laid on the floor as a temporary measure. Pupils working within the loop receive audio programmes without being inhibited

by connected wires (the headsets are cordless). The system therefore, has particular advantages, especially with multi-handicapped children, either individually or in groups; or where instructions for practical tasks are being relayed. These special tasks may well be audio-typing, throwing a pot, using a lathe, etc. In these circumstances a foot control for the tape recorder will enable the pupil to pace himself. Another particular advantage with the audio-link system is that the pupil can still be taught in the noisiest of places. The tape recorder can also be used in conjunction with slides or film strips—using a synchronising unit.

5 A development of the tape recorder is an *instrument of the nature of the language master*. It is compact, light and with all parts, even microphone, built-in. The 2-track is inset in a strip along the bottom of a card. On one track the teacher records. This is played back by the pupil, who then, by means of a simple rocker switch, can record his own attempt on the other track. He can make as many attempts as he wishes, and listen time and again to the teacher. It is not possible for the pupil to erase the teacher's voice. The teacher writes on the card, above the tape, the word, words, or sentences which are recorded, and the machine has many applications, from picture-word recognition, teaching of reading, languages, etc.

6 A further innovation with the 4-track tape recorder is to utilise it as an *audio-response teaching machine*. A ' magic box ' enables the instructional material to be heard, and an auditory response to be made without damaging the original programme material. The original material is recorded by the teacher on track 1 of the tape, leaving spaces for the pupil's responses where appropriate. The machine is then set in the record position on track 3. The pupil has only to operate the pause button on the recorder. He can make auditory or written responses as instructed, for the ' magic box ' enables him to listen to track 1 and record on track 3. The pupil is actively engaged in listening and responding during the entire period of instruction.

7 Where much recording is done in a school it is almost essential to have a machine whereby tapes can be cleared of recorded material at great speed. The clearing is done by magnetic means in this machine, in a matter of seconds.

8 There is a number of excellent *projectors* most suitable for use with partially sighted children. Nearly all pose a problem of projection, however, and this problem must be solved first. Partially sighted children need to get close to the screen in order to see sufficiently well. With normal projection methods, the pupils will be in the way of the beam. The only satisfactory solution is to use back-projection. Manufactured screens are expensive, and few are sufficiently large. They can be made quite simply, however, even from a tea chest, using a mirror within at 45 degrees, and a panel of pearl grey plastic sheet, $\frac{1}{4}$" thick, let into one side. Bigger and more sophisticated ones can be made by the more handy teacher, using ply or blockboard.

9 A good 16mm *talkie projector* is a great asset. Lenses are available with all makes, for use with back projection. There are many sources from which 16mm films can be borrowed free, and a really good range of subjects is covered. 8mm projectors are excellent, too, particularly for use with films made by the school. The enterprising can write and produce excellent 8mm films. These are

K*

of particular value to the children, for the subject matter is selected to fit them instead of the curriculum being altered to fit borrowed films. Film can be stripped, and spoken commentary added, which greatly increases the value.

10 The *overhead projector* has special significance for the partially sighted. It has a great variety of applications, and its delight is that material can be added through overlays by both teacher and pupil, whilst projecting. The teacher faces the pupils during the projection, and interest can be constantly maintained. The teacher at all times remains the integral part of the group and is in an ideal position to pace the lesson properly, to revive flagging interest and to involve the pupils in the activity. Use of the projector can be made in the teaching of writing to partially sighted pupils. A fallacy is that partially sighted children write badly because of their severe loss of vision. Whilst in some cases this is true, in the majority of cases it is not so. The chief cause of the bad writing is, basically, that the children have never seen letters and words whilst under construction. They have seen only the completed product, and have been obliged to find a way of copying this The overhead projector solves this problem. The teacher constructs the letters and words on the projector and the children can see this throughout the course of construction. The machine is valuable in science teaching, whether simple or advanced; magnetism, ripple tank, etc., can be demonstrated in movement. Using transparencies, either commercial or made by the school, the machine has a firm place in the teaching of number concepts, geography, music, technical drawing, mathematics, etc., etc.

11 *Slide projectors* are most useful additions to audio-visual aids for the partially sighted. 35mm transparencies on a variety of subjects can be bought. The ideal, however, is for transparencies to be prepared by members of the school. Blank transparencies are available for completion, and drawings, illustrations, maps, etc. can be photographed as required; by careful selection a teacher can build up a programme exactly suited to the pupil's needs. Certain machines can take circular magazines holding up to 100 slides, so that one is not restricted to the normal 36.

12 *Slide tapes* can then be produced as a natural development. A slide tape is a 35mm sequence with a tape recorded soundtrack, so synchronised that a signal on the tape changes the slide on the projector; presentation is automatic. The slide tape is just about the most inexpensive method of automatic presentation. Slides can be recorded or substituted, and tapes can be spliced or re-recorded. Out-of-date slides can be replaced and, using only one set of slides, several tape recordings can be made and used with them, depending on the age and intelligence of the audience. The slide tape is an excellent and flexible audio-visual device for the teacher and possesses considerable advantages over the film strip or motion picture.

MOBILITY TRAINING

Mobility training is so important that more information about it may be useful than could appropriately be given in the section on Physical Education in paragraphs 7.50–7.56.

A Mobility training for the blind

1 Parents and teachers of blind children must help them to acquire :

  (a) Awareness of their own bodies and their relationship with other people in space. This sense of orientation, sometimes called the kinesthetic sense, is often lacking in blind people and is vital to them, particularly to those engaged in the profession of physiotherapy.

  (b) Good balance and a natural fluency of movement of the different limbs and of the whole body. This will not of itself happen in the blind who, for example, may try to protect themselves by holding their arms stiffly in front of them and may walk flat-footed to avoid a twist on a kerb or uneven stone. They often, presumably because of freedom from fear, move more fluently when swimming than walking or running.

  (c) Correct muscular development and in consequence good posture and gait. Blind children have a well known tendency to bad posture and physical mannerisms.

  (d) The health, confidence and independence which come from proper bodily development and fluency of movement.

2 The ability of blind people to orientate themselves by use of direct sounds and echoes has always been admired by the sighted, who in the past did not feel competent to provide a methodical training in mobility because for them sight was the dominant sense. Use of a short white stick was considered necessary simply to warn others, including motorists, to avoid a collision with blind people, but many blind felt that use of such a stick made them conspicuous and humiliated them.

3 After the 1939–45 war a different outlook emerged. In the USA a serious attempt was made methodically to train men blinded in the war to travel unescorted whether on foot or by public transport. It came to be realised—as indeed many blind people had known before—that a stick can valuably be used for detecting obstacles and for creating echoes. After training with the long cane, as it came to be called, blind travellers no longer tried to be inconspicuous (in consequence creating a hazard or arousing pity) but sought to be conspicuously competent, gaining independence and freedom through their skill.

4 The long cane is not the only aid to mobility, for blind people should learn to use and depend on a variety of aids. Blind adults are taught to handle and direct guide dogs. In 1962 for the first time in this country Dr. (now Professor) L. Kay and the late Dr J. A. Leonard tested in a school setting the ultra-sonic aid sponsored by St Dunstan's. Testing and training still continue with the most

recently developed version called the Binaural Sensor. A major problem of these aids is the difficulty for the user in distinguishing between relevant and irrelevant information received.

5 But the need for long cane training of blind people young enough to learn has been almost universally accepted. A National Mobility Centre has been established in Birmingham by the Royal National Institute for the Blind, St Dunstan's and the Birmingham Royal Institution for the Blind, mainly at present for the training of instructors. Training in long cane techniques and mobility generally, including a preliminary training for children before they take the long cane training, is recognised as a necessary part of the curriculum of each school for the blind. Acquisition of skill in mobility is not only an educational asset. It may in later life make the difference between holding down and failing to cope with a job, for example in piano tuning or welfare work.

6 The technique of long cane usage is briefly this: the cane is held centrally in front of the body and is swung gently from side to side. It covers an arc just wider than the shoulders and touches the ground in time with the step opposite to the side on which the point of the stick is placed. In addition to detecting obstacles the cane supplies the user with a variety of information about his passage and whereabouts.

7 The training has to be individual and takes as long as 60 hours. The blind trainee is taught to make use of all possible clues—aural, tactile and olfactory. He learns what obstacles he will meet and how he can best negotiate them. He steers a straight course, not natural to people without sight*. He learns how to use a map in raised relief, especially in planning a journey. He acquires skill in exercising courtesy and in knowing how best to receive help from sighted people. He uses public transport with confidence. He moves competently in a room or shop. He adopts a proper posture and learns deportment.

8 Teachers have given much thought to mobility training, encouraged and advised by Dr Leonard, who established the Blind Mobility Research Unit at Nottingham University. A meeting of teachers led to the setting up of a working party, which reported in 1968†, and notes of further meetings of teachers have been published‡. Much work is being undertaken on production of raised relief maps for mobility training; pamphlets are also issued for the instruction of parents.

9 Teachers know that there are many questions still to be answered about mobility training for children: the exact nature of preliminary training before a long cane training is attempted; the ages at which different children should start a full training and the degree of intelligence required of a child undertaking the complete course; the problems of training children with residual vision or additional handicap; the best ways of giving experience (see Section B on mobility training for the partially sighted); education in use of maps, and the best lines and symbols to be employed.

---

* Movement and Spatial Awareness in Blind Children and Youth: Bryan J. Cratty (Charles C· Thomas, Springfield, Illinois, 1971).

† Mobility Guidelines (Nottingham University Printing and Photography Unit, 1968).

‡ The Teacher of the Blind (Pamphlet on Mobility Training in schools for the visually handicapped, 1971).

B Mobility training for the partially sighted

1 Mobility training for the partially sighted should begin at as early an age as possible. If severely partially sighted children are to develop fully it is essential that advice to parents from the earliest stage should include knowledge of a carefully structured programme related to the needs and environment of each child. Even in the early months of life the children should be exposed to a wide variety of sensory experiences, though care must be taken not to confuse them with too many unrelated activities. They need, at all stages, to be able to synthesize and correlate the impressions they are receiving—impressions which because they may be ill-defined, distorted or inaccurately perceived could well lead to the development of faulty or superficial concepts. It is of considerable value in this connection if the adult caring for the young partially sighted child carries out a running commentary on new activities as these are undertaken, verbalising and exploring the point and purpose of what is taking place. For example, fathers, when servicing the car, could deliberately enumerate the stages in checking air pressure in tyres and connecting the foot pump. Mother, when making a cake, could comment as she cracks the eggs and carries out the mixing process.

2 Mobility at the stage of entry to the infant school should be closely linked with visual training. Large wheeled toys and tricycles, scooters, trucks and engines, which are manipulated by the children's use of the whole body movement, can play a useful part in increasing confidence and spatial knowledge. Where children have been over-protected or otherwise restricted by an unfavourable environment, it is important that they are encouraged from the beginning towards the achievement of independence and responsibility in the school and classroom situation. It is often necessary where development has been severely retarded to take them through the stages which have been missed in the earlier years. In addition to self-help in the sphere of dressing, feeding, washing and toilet training, they should be shown how to use and care for and replace all the toys, materials and items of equipment which are found in the infant classroom. It is on the basis of this type of training in these early years that future development will take place; for it is only by fully comprehending and exploring the possibilities inherent in their immediate surroundings that children with severely defective vision will reach their ultimate potential. Left to themselves they will all too often curtail and circumscribe their experiences, and fail to develop the curiosity and desire for adventure which is natural to un-handicapped children.

3 Every opportunity should be taken in and out of school to expand the range of activities in which the children can confidently take part. Sand and water play, dressing up, the acting out of situations in the Wendy House, all types of movement games using the resources of the school building, the playground and, if one is available, a learner swimming pool, should be introduced to the children at this stage. Simple errands and messages making use of the different locations within the school should be undertaken. Local walks, accompanied by an adult who can draw attention and interpret in a way that is of value to the children, can gradually be extended to visits further afield around home and school. Shopping expeditions to buy a specific item for classroom or home use or to a self-service store, where the children can choose and collect goods from the shelves, can lead to simple excursions with a clear cut objective. Railway stations, farms, parks, workshops, fire stations, Zoos, airports, har-

bours and building sites, wherever available, can provide much in the way of stimulus and experience. Visits of this kind are a desirable feature in the programme of any infant school; they are vitally necessary for partially sighted children at this age.

4 Training in mobility in the later primary stage is really an extension of the infant programme in ways that are commensurate with the children's growing abilities and independence. Opportunities should be provided for the children to initiate and plan both individual and group activities based on topics arising within the school curriculum. Children with normal vision will automatically progress to this but some partially sighted children, particularly where they are late entrants to the school, may need help in doing so. Group games and expressive free work in drama have particular value. Modern trends in physical education, where uninhibited movement is used by children to explore the relationship of their body to the space around them, can be linked with music and natural rhythm. There is an additional need, in a physical education programme designed for the partially sighted, for structured remedial movement based on individual needs to be provided. Children's attention should be drawn to observing particular features and hazards of the environment. Practice in road safety training and the inculcation of confidence in the use of public transport now loom large. Training of this kind involves much patient practice. The further extension of visits to libraries, factories, museums, theatres—and ultimately to journeys taken in groups to other parts of the country—provides an opportunity for correlation with realistic everyday experiences. Shopping activities, surveys, observation games and programmes of exploration can be undertaken by the children independently at the close of the primary stage; school and home should work together to ensure that sufficient time is devoted to this.

5 As the children progress through the secondary stage, there should be ample opportunity for the development of individual mobility outside the protected area of school and home. The physical education programme can now include many of the games and pursuits available to young people with normal vision even if some modification is necessary and the achievement of competitive standards is not possible. Few restrictions are necessary, other than those imposed by delicate sight or where imperfect vision creates a danger for the player or fellow participant. It is possible by carefully planning the physical education programme to see that no boy or girl is excluded from an activity which is patently worthwhile. Adult supervision should become more and more curtailed in external activities in progressive stages, until by the end of school life all young people should feel confident in the use of all types of public transport likely to be available to them and ready to tackle any demands which adult society imposes upon them. It is helpful if regular attendance at other schools, colleges or recreational institutes, on either a day release or an evening class basis, can be arranged in the final months at school. This enables the partially sighted boy or girl to meet and overcome problems of mobility, location and social adjustment while still in a position to seek skilled advice. Participation should be encouraged in community service activities in the Duke of Edinburgh's Award Scheme, in exchange visits with schools and individuals at home and abroad, and in school expeditions which impose real demands on the initiative and endurance of partially sighted adolescents.

144

6 It is often necessary to offer guidance and counselling to parents at this stage, since it may be difficult for them to make the final step in conceding independence to a handicapped teenage son or daughter. Part-time employment at the weekends or in holiday periods gives useful practice in adjusting to complex work relationships and in developing a positive attitude to adult working life. The young people should be helped to find the way appropriate to their individual handicap of dealing with the mechanics of everyday living—slot machines, train indicators, cash registers, escalators, price labels and size tags, recognition of street names, interview techniques, form-filling and all the multifarious gadgets and activities which will challenge their competence in modern society. The provision of an additional inconspicuous low visual aid is sometimes helpful at this stage; and it is often re-assuring to the adolescent if it is made apparent that the most adequate adult often finds himself in a situation in which he needs help or guidance. It is at this time above all else that the earlier training in mobility and the fostering of positive attitudes to new situations really bears fruit. There is no substitute for the patient exploration of individual capabilities.

SURVEY OF TEACHERS

Statistical information was invited from headteachers and teachers in schools and assessment centres for the blind and in schools and units for the partially sighted. The response was full enough to provide data from which reliable conclusions could be drawn. Though the letter and questionnaire were sent out in the early stages of the Committee's work it is likely that the general situation remains the same.

On the basis of this statistical information, two of our members have assessed the position in relation to teaching staff in schools for each handicap. The points they have picked out for comment differ somewhat but, in order to facilitate comparisons, statistical tables have, where possible, been combined and the two surveys, while kept separate, have been rearranged under the same pattern of headings.

The statistical tables (Section 1) provide information, for both the blind and the partially sighted, about the numbers of teachers, their sex, age, length of service, moves or attempted moves in the past 5 years and membership of a professional organisation. The commentaries (Sections 2 and 3) follow this order :

    Stability, qualifications and previous experience
    Mobility and prospects of promotion
    Short courses and contact with teachers in other schools.

Section 3 contains two additional tables showing the career experience of assistant and head teachers in schools for the partially sighted. At the end there is a note on blind teachers in schools for the blind (Section 4).

STATISTICAL TABLES FOR TEACHERS OF THE BLIND AND THE PARTIALLY SIGHTED

	Blind	Partially sighted
Numbers of full-time staff answering questionnaires	200	204
Sex : Male	49%	34%
Female	51%	66%
Ages : Under 30	25%	21%
31–40	29%	25%
41–50	24%	26%
50+	22%	28%
Length of service in present school: 5 years or less	45%	46%
6–14 years	32%	39%
15 years or more	23%	15%
Moved to teach elsewhere in past 5 years	28%	21%
Attempted to move unsuccessfully in past 5 years	15%	16%
Membership of professional organisation :		
College of Teachers of the Blind	60%	2%
Association for the Education of the Partially Sighted	—	24%
Association for Special Education	16%	33%
Specialist subject	23%	10%

COMMENTARY ON STAFFING IN SCHOOLS AND ASSESSMENT CENTRES FOR THE BLIND

Stability, qualifications and previous experience

1 There is no doubt that there is stability of staff in the schools for the blind. In view of the closure of the Bristol School for the Blind and the decrease in numbers of young blind children, together with the relatively small numbers of teachers leaving the schools, it is unlikely that there is a shortage. No head teacher has mentioned one. This stability may be due to a sense of vocation; to an unwillingness to drop salary if a move is made without promotion; to an inability to move either because of inadequate qualification and experience or to a difficulty in persuading employers that experience in a school for the blind is generally valuable. It may also be due to a combination of any of these. There seems no doubt from a study of the details that there is a strong sense of vocation among the teachers. Many have come after full experience in other educational fields, not from sentimentality, but from a wish to be in a situation where there is a strong need for welfare and where patient work is needed to enable the child to participate happily and to achieve real progress. Two head teachers have commented on the long hours worked by many members of staff to provide outside activities and pastoral care for pupils in a fully residential situation. Wives and friends also give a great deal of help. All head teachers would endorse these comments.

Mobility and prospects of promotion

2 It does seem, however, that schools for the blind are looked on as very much outside the mainstream not only of education generally, but of education in the special schools. One headmaster comments that experience in a school for the blind is of no help in an application for promotion to a senior post in another form of school, including a school for the partially-sighted. This attitude is found if applicants try for posts in schools for the educationally sub-normal or physically handicapped, despite the fact that many of the psychological and temperamental difficulties to be found among blind pupils must be very much the same as those to be encountered in pupils suffering from other forms of handicap. One writer comments wistfully that conscientiousness can even hamper a teacher's chances, as it is left out of account and only qualifications and apparently relevant experience are considered. It is probable that the specialist teacher can move on more easily to other educational fields, whether from one of the grammar schools or from a technical post at an assessment centre. Yet one deputy-head of a secondary school comments that a move involving promotion is difficult to achieve; and that to move without promotion is a hard decision for a young married teacher to make, since it entails a drop in salary and probably less good housing and living facilities. It is likely, as one head points out, that the teacher in a school for the blind with other handicaps is in a better position to move within the sphere of special education.

3 Writers comment on the difficulty of achieving promotion within the schools for the blind. It is a very small area and appointments are scarce. One male

member of staff in a primary school comments on the fact that initial dedication can wear thin after several years if a teacher finds that he cannot progress up a ladder either within his own school or outside it. There is relatively little promotion even to posts in other schools for the blind. Often senior posts in these go to applicants from outside. The deputy head of a secondary school for the blind notes that teachers generally well qualified for a headship or deputy headship may feel diffident about applying for senior posts in primary schools because they lack experience of dealing with children of a younger age. It is particularly difficult for women to achieve promotion outside the Sunshine Home schools. Only two other schools have headmistresses. This trend is present, of course, in normal education, since it is usual for the head of a comprehensive school to be a man, certainly if it is, as commonly, a co-educational school.

Short courses and contact with teachers in other schools

4 While heads visit each other's schools fairly frequently, assistant teachers do not often do so. Teachers in the secondary schools for the blind may link with their opposite numbers in the same subjects. Teachers meet at branch meetings of the College of Teachers of the Blind, but the subject-matter at these meetings is often of greater interest to the social welfare officer of the blind than to the school teacher. A healthy and valuable development in recent years has been the holding of subject meetings in schools—on domestic science, physical education, mathematics, science, methods of producing embossed diagrams. It is hoped that finance and time can be found to enable these sectional meetings to continue. There is no doubt that the week-end courses organised by the Department of Education and Science have not only been of very great value for their content and their educational stimulus, but have brought together for friendship and interchange of ideas a wide group of teachers and members of the Department, who could not otherwise have met, certainly not in conditions free from other preoccupation. It is hoped that these can be maintained and that as many teachers as possible can be enabled to take part in them. The Department of Education at Birmingham University now provides a course for teachers of the partially sighted as well as of the blind. In the two all-age schools for the blind and partially sighted combined, the staff of course associate closely. Otherwise evidence reveals very little contact at present between members of staff of the schools for the blind and those of the partially-sighted, even between the head teachers of these schools. Recently there have been efforts to improve communications between the College of Teachers of the Blind and the Association for the Education of the Partially-sighted, to which in any case only a small proportion of teachers of the partially sighted belong.

5 It is difficult to assess how much contact there is between teaching staff in the schools for the blind and the normal schools in the country. Yet there is a considerable spill-over from the methods and ideas of normal education into the education of the blind. It is vital that teachers in the schools for the blind should be in close touch with development in the normal schools. In some matters teachers of the visually handicapped have their special contribution to make. Specialist teachers take pupils to Society meetings in other schools and attend occasional courses. This can happen more easily in a city than in a country area, particularly when distances between schools are small. Head

teachers of secondary schools no doubt do their best to attend meetings of professional associations, thereby keeping in touch and gaining valuable friendships which may often lead to co-operation between sighted schools and the schools for the blind. Heads also have involvements of other kinds in local affairs. But it may not be so easy for assistant teachers to make contact. One teacher in a Sunshine Home school comments that it is difficult to keep abreast of recent developments in normal education and suggests various methods, such as courses and visits, to remedy this situation. Yet many teachers, particularly perhaps those in maintained schools and in cities, no doubt have wide contacts.

COMMENTARY ON STAFFING IN SCHOOLS FOR THE PARTIALLY SIGHTED

Stability, qualifications and previous experience

1 The length of time spent by assistant teachers in ordinary teaching and teaching in other special schools is shown below. The comparatively large number of those who have undertaken service in other fields of special education and in ordinary schools is perhaps indicative of the generalised approach of the teacher of the partially sighted to his career. It is likely that the teacher of the partially sighted sees himself as less of a specialist teacher than does his colleague in schools for the blind and this is to some extent indicated by the number who evince interest in teaching in other areas of special education in answer to a later question. It will be noted that a small number of teachers had entered schools for the partially sighted without teaching experience in other types of school and in each case cross checking revealed that this was the first appointment.

Length of time spent in :	Nil	Under 5 yrs.	5–15 yrs.	15+ yrs.
Ordinary schools	11%	40%	34%	15%
Other special schools	64%	15%	19%	2%

2 The majority of assistant teachers in schools for the partially sighted are qualified non-graduate teachers. Only nine of the schools have one or more graduate teachers on the staff. Six schools have one only, two schools have two, and one has twelve. Twelve per cent of those teaching in schools for the partially sighted are graduates compared with 8·5% of those in all special schools and 21·2% of those in all schools in the maintained or direct grant category. Only 13% of the teachers had undertaken supplementary training relating to a general or specific handicap and a further 5% have taken an additional qualification in a specialist subject. No figures for comparison are directly available but over 20% of those working in the field of special education as a whole have taken one year supplementary courses in the past five years alone. It is likely that the absence, until recently, of a specific qualification in the field of partially sighted teaching has militated against a larger number of teachers seeking additional qualifications. Of those who are qualified to teach the blind (10%), only two are working in schools where both the blind and partially sighted are not jointly catered for.

3 The pattern revealed in the answers of the head teachers differed from that shown in the answers of assistant teachers to an extent which indicated that separate analysis of their replies would be useful. Twenty-five head teachers of partially sighted schools and schools containing partially sighted units replied. Fifteen of these were in the 50+ age group, 8 were aged between 40 and 50 and 2 were under 40. Fifteen of the head teachers were men and 10 were women. The

following table relates the career experience of the head teachers and shows the very high percentage who have served in their present schools for more than 15 years.

	Nil	Under 5	5–15	More than 15 years
Ordinary schools	16%	48%	36%	Nil
Other special schools	32%	40%	8%	20%
PS Schools	—	12%*	16%	72%
Present school	—	16%	28%	56%

*all in units in schools for other types of children

Four of the head teachers were graduates. Only 2 head teachers had undertaken a course in teaching the handicapped, but 4 had diplomas in child development, advanced education or sociology.

4 Nearly 60% of assistant teachers indicated that they would welcome the opportunity to take a course giving a qualification in teaching the partially sighted, with a slightly greater number specifying that they would be prepared to do so on a part-time basis only than expressed willingness to do so as a full-time student or without expressing a preference. Of the 40% who indicated that they would not be prepared to take such a course, about 10% expressed the conviction that such a course was not necessary, about 32% made it clear that they did not intend to stay in partially sighted teaching indefinitely and almost 50% that they would find it difficult for personal or domestic reasons. Of the remainder in this category the reason most commonly advanced was imminent or approaching retirement. Fourteen head teachers were not prepared to undertake a course relating to the education of the visually handicapped and most gave as their reason their approaching retirement; 11 were prepared to do so.

Mobility and prospects of promotion
5 Of the 43 teachers who had successfully changed their post during the past five years only five were in partially sighted teaching at the beginning of that period so that the change was from another type of school into the partially sighted field, not within the area of partially sighted teaching. Of the 32 who had tried unsuccessfully to change their post 24 had been in their present school more than five years. About 40% of the teachers had at some time contemplated working with children with other handicaps, but it was not possible to be sure whether what was referred to in answer to this question was in some cases previous service in other special schools. Twenty-six had contemplated work with ESN children, 19 with physically handicapped, 10 with maladjusted, only 6 with the blind, and a few with autistic, delicate or hospitalised children. Comparative figures are not available but it may well be that there is less mobility among teachers of the partially sighted than among teachers in ordinary schools.

152

6 All except fourteen teachers felt that promotion in the partially sighted field was comparatively restricted and this view was strongly held by those who already carried posts of responsibility. In fact the percentage of teachers who have been awarded some kind of additional payment in this form is not very much lower in schools for the partially sighted than in ordinary schools—the difference being in the order of 2–3%. The head teachers were unanimous in their opinion that promotion in schools for the partially sighted is restricted.

Short courses and contact with teachers in other schools

7 Just under a third indicated that they had attended a short course designed for teachers of the visually handicapped, but since the questionnaire was completed before the onset of the latest series of DES courses for teachers of the partially sighted it is likely that a much higher proportion have now done so. Nearly 80% of those who had attended short courses of this kind had done so on one or more occasions under the auspices of the DES. Nearly 60% had attended short courses in subjects or areas not directly connected with partially sighted teaching and these ranged widely across the entire field of teaching interests, with modern mathematics, reading and handicrafts predominating. All the head teachers except 2 recently appointed had attended short courses in the teaching of the partially sighted, and two-thirds had attended short courses in other fields.

BLIND TEACHERS IN SCHOOLS FOR THE BLIND

We made particular enquiry about the blind teachers, of whom there were thirty-six in the schools for the blind. Most of these have stayed in the same school, at least after the onset of blindness if they have gone blind in adult life. They have a valuable contribution to make, though, because of the need for teachers to help blind children with so many practical things, there is a limit to the number of blind teachers that any one school can absorb. Some do not always find their teaching and discipline easy. They may have to cope with the written work of a partially-sighted child. It may be hard for them to obtain access to new material and they perhaps tend to rely more than the sighted teacher on the material and methods they built up themselves during their training and early years of teaching. Whereas sighted children may exercise consideration for a teacher's handicap, blind children have no such inhibitions in their attitude to a blind teacher. Handling blind children is often a tiring business and blind teachers may find it particularly exhausting. As with any teacher, if he loses heart, the game is up. He has to rise continually to meet each new surge of young vitality. Many blind teachers remain throughout their careers fully capable of meeting this continual challenge.

The following points of interest emerged from the enquiry :

1 Twelve of the 36 whole-time and part-time teachers can read print, even if with difficulty or using a low visual aid.

2 Two teach music, two piano tuning.

3 Eight received further education at an establishment for blind students; of these, five seem to have had additional training in centres where they were working with normally sighted students.

4 The training and qualifications of the 36 teachers are at least comparable with those of fully sighted teachers. It is rather easier now for blind students to be accepted at Institutes and Colleges of Education than it was a few years ago.

5 Many have clearly tried to obtain additional qualifications.

6 Previous experience is limited, except for teachers blinded in later life.

7 Once in a school for the blind, they have tended to stay.

8 Generally speaking blind teachers seem rarely to attend refresher courses.

Printed in England for Her Majesty's Stationery Office by James Townsend & Sons Ltd., Exeter.

Dd 507366 K40 10/72